WHAT PEOPLE ARE SAYING ABOUT

The CATHOLIC BRIEFCASE

Practical and powerful! Wherever you are in your spiritual journey, I think you will benefit tremendously from reading this book.
—**Matthew Kelly**, founder of DynamicCatholic.com and author of *Rediscovering Catholicism*

Many people feel that they have to put down their faith when they pick up their briefcase. But *The Catholic Briefcase* teaches us how to carry both. With practical tips on how to integrate our Catholicism with our careers, we learn how our faith can make us better business people—and how our jobs can make us saints.
—**Matthew Warner** of FallibleBlogma.com and CEO of flockNote

Faith-filled practicing Catholics will be affirmed, renewed, and uplifted as they do their best to apply Catholic principles at the office. Those beginning their journey will receive sound advice and will come away with a clear understanding of the true harmony that exists between faith and work.
—**Teresa Tomeo**, syndicated Catholic talk-show host, motivational speaker, and best-selling Catholic author

Do you want to be a better spouse, a better provider, a person filled with joy and gratitude? Then open up *The Catholic Briefcase* by Randy Hain to learn about the secrets for living a life that successfully balances and integrates both faith and work. Stop imagining the perfect job and start living it!
—**Dr. Bill Thierfelder**, president of Belmont Abbey College

Whether your workplace is the courtroom or the kitchen, Wall Street or the corner market, *The Catholic Briefcase* belongs on your reading list....Randy Hain offers real-world scenarios and shines light on scores of Catholics who strive to balance saintliness and productivity. With measurable suggestions, reflection, and discussion prompts, written in a motivational tone, *The Catholic Briefcase* will inspire you all seven days of the week to more fully live out your vocation with joy and passion.

> —**Lisa M. Hendey**, founder and editor,
> CatholicMom.com, and author of
> *A Book of Saints for Catholic Moms*

The recommendations in this book are absolutely achievable....It is a very practical guide to fusing faith and work.

> —**Anthony Lynch**, business development executive,
> Systems Alliance, Inc.

Randy gives clear and concise insights into integrating faith and work so each will blossom more fully. Each chapter features tools, reflections, and recommendations that are easy to understand and apply. I recommend this book to all Catholics interested in using their God-given gifts and specific talents to their fullest potential to glorify God and serve others.

> —**Tom Peterson**, president and founder,
> CatholicsComeHome.org

The strength of *The Catholic Briefcase* is in its practicality. Randy not only lays out guiding principles for integrating faith and work, he also does an excellent job of exploring tangible ways to live those principles in the daily grind....Buy it, read it, give it to a coworker, and buy it again!

> —**Matt Swaim,** producer, *The Son Rise Morning
> Show* on EWTN Radio, author of *The Eucharist
> and the Rosary* and *Prayer in the Digital Age*

Randy has prescribed an excellent road map for Catholic leadership. Writing in a straightforward style, he leads you on an exploration of faith and work. This is a book that will help Catholic business professionals recalibrate their compass.

—**Joe George**, senior executive
of a technology company

The Catholic Briefcase offers every Catholic helpful insights in navigating the complex and sometimes difficult challenges to integrating our work and faith lives.

—**Phillip M. Thompson,** JD, PhD, LLM,
executive director, Aquinas Center of Theology
at Emory University

While some Catholic professionals might struggle with the integration of their faith and their work, my bet is that many more of us just don't think about it at all. Randy has given us good reasons to not only reflect on how we see ourselves in the business community, he has assembled the tools to help us take our first steps as well!

—**Allan J. DeNiro,** senior vice president and
chief people officer, Haverty's Furniture Company

The Catholic Briefcase is a must-read for anyone struggling with how to balance our "work" with our "life's work."

—**Kimberly Samon,** senior executive
at a major manufacturing company

…In *The Catholic Briefcase,* Randy Hain deftly explains how you can integrate the whole of your life—your love for God, your faith, family, growth in virtue, business conduct, friendships, financial decisions, leisure activities, etc.—into a mature, integrated, and well-ordered continuum…

—**Patrick Madrid,** (patrickmadrid.com),
director of the Envoy Institute of Belmont Abbey
College, author of *Search and Rescue,* and host of
the Thursday edition of EWTN Radio's "Open
Line" broadcast (3 to 5 p.m. ET).

The
CATHOLIC
BRIEFCASE

The CATHOLIC BRIEFCASE

TOOLS FOR INTEGRATING FAITH AND WORK

Randy Hain

FOREWORD BY PATRICK LENCIONI

Liguori
LIGUORI, MISSOURI

Imprimi Potest:
Harry Grile, CSsR, Provincial
Denver Province, The Redemptorists

Published by Liguori Publications
Liguori, Missouri 63057

To order, call 800-325-9521, or visit liguori.org

Library of Congress Cataloging-in-Publication Data

Hain, Randy.
    The Catholic briefcase : practical tools for integrating faith and work / by Randy Hain ; foreword by Patrick Lencioni.—1st ed.
        p. cm.
    Includes bibliographical references.
    ISBN 978-0-7648-2052-6 (alk. paper)
    1. Work—Religious aspects—Catholic Church. 2. Catholic Church—Doctrines. 3. Employees—Religious life. I. Title.
    BX1795.W67H35 2011
    248.8'8—dc23

                                                                            2011038931

Liguori Publications, a nonprofit corporation, is an apostolate of the Redemptorists. To learn more about the Redemptorists, visit Redemptorists.com.

Printed in the United States of America
15 14 13 12 11 / 5 4 3 2
First Edition

In loving memory of my mother,
Sandi Hain.
Her wonderful example of faith, love, and selflessness
inspired all who knew her.

Contents

CONTENTS

Acknowledgments

OVER THE LAST FEW YEARS I have felt a growing desire to write a book on the subject of integrating faith and work. When Liguori Publications called me right after Thanksgiving 2010 with the same idea, that desire became a reality. I appreciate this opportunity to, I hope, shed a little light on one particular and largely ignored area where our Catholic faith is desperately needed: the workplace.

Writing this book was a labor of love, but it took discipline to finish it amidst my various other responsibilities. However, no book is truly written alone. I am blessed to have a number of people in my life who contributed something special to this project. The members of my Woodstock Business Conference group are an ongoing source of inspiration for me, and I am proud to know all of these fine Catholic business leaders. Their experiences had a great influence on my thinking as I wrote this book. I am very grateful to Lisa Guthrie of Grammar She Wrote and Lisa Tilt for their friendship and expert editing help. Matt Tovrog, Cathy Perry, Tom Peterson, Theresa Thomas, and Andy Hepburn also chipped in with helpful editing tips to improve the book and boundless enthusiasm for the project. It takes confidence to put your thoughts on paper for public consumption, but also a lot of humility to let your friends tear it to shreds.

The word "gratitude" doesn't do justice to how I feel toward Jennifer Baugh, Paige Barry, Dr. Paul Voss, Terry Trout, David McCullough, David Murphy, Andrew Mangione, Charlie Douglas, and Alex Muñoz for their candid insights and fearless examples of living out their Catholic faith in the workplace. This book would not be possible without their selfless contributions.

I want to thank five of my favorite authors, whose writing has long inspired me to be a better Catholic, a better man, a better husband, a better father, and a better leader. Thank you to Pat Lencioni, Dr. Peter Kreeft, Chris Lowney, Jim Nolan, and Dr. Michael Naughton.

Price Harding, Glen Jackson, Dr. Ron Young, Dan Stotz, Dr. Phil Thompson, Lorraine Murray, Matt Swaim, the entire team at Bell Oaks, Cathy Bickerstaff, Ken Davison, my father, Steve Hain, and countless others…thank you for the incredible support and encouragement.

Deacon Mike Bickerstaff is a friend, mentor, and a frequent collaborator on ministry work related to promoting faith in the workplace. We also cofounded the popular *Integrated Catholic Life* e-magazine (integratedcatholiclife.org) in early 2010 to promote our passion for serving Christ and promoting the concept of the integrated life. His encouragement and ideas for the book were incredibly helpful in getting it completed.

My wife, Sandra, and our sons, Alex and Ryan, were a great encouragement in this process, and I thank God every day that I am blessed with such a wonderful family. Thank you from the bottom of my heart.

Most important, I give thanks to our Lord and pray that he will be glorified through this book, and that people will draw closer to him by living as faithful Catholics in the workplace.

Foreword

LET'S BE HONEST. It's easy to look at a book like this one and think, "I probably don't need to read that right now."

After all, when we're working hard just to understand and live our Catholic faith in our personal lives, we can easily justify the postponement of trying to integrate it into our work. It's not that we don't think it would be a good thing to do some day, just not right now. I can hear myself saying, "I'll get to that as soon as I get my faith life squared away personally."

Well, here's the thing, and it's one of the most important lessons I learned from Randy Hain in this book: I am not going to get my faith life squared away personally until I make it the center of my life in every way, including at work. I can no more justify keeping my faith out of my job than I can my marriage, my family, or my Sunday Mass. As it turns out, being Catholic is as much a noun as it is a verb, which means I am not meant to simply "practice" my faith at certain times, but to "be" it all the time.

But rest assured, fully integrating our faith with our work is not nearly as uncomfortable as it seems. In fact, it's the most natural, comfortable, and logical thing we can do. That's because it's not about going out and taking a public stand and pushing people mired in a secular world out of their comfort zones. At least not at first.

Most of what it requires is a simple, but profound, internal change, one that will entail some private behavioral adjustments. Eventually, through these small and wonderful changes in our daily lives, our perspective on our faith will shift profoundly and we will find ourselves quietly witnessing to Christ in even the smallest details of our work. We will gradually emanate his love in ways that will make those around us wonder, and maybe even ask us, why we are the way we are. And trust me, when that happens we'll find it easy to witness to our faith, out of quiet confidence and love, not fear or defensiveness.

I must admit that my affinity for this book is not attributable solely to its content. Knowing who wrote it drives my enthusiasm for it, as it should for any work. Randy Hain has been a role model for me, and many others like me, in gracefully, lovingly, confidently living his faith at work. His discipline and commitment to his faith as well as his business makes me want to be a better person, a better Christian, a better Catholic in every way. He has confronted me around some of the most important, and difficult, subjects, and provoked me to take steps in my faith life that I wouldn't have done otherwise. And he has never, ever made me feel less than him along the way.

I guess that's the thing about a great book. It works not only because the content makes so much sense, but because the author has been living that content himself. I pray that you will benefit from Randy's encouragement as much as I have.

PATRICK LENCIONI, PRESIDENT,

THE TABLE GROUP;

AUTHOR, *THE FIVE DYSFUNCTIONS OF A TEAM*

INTRODUCTION

Why Do We Leave Our Faith at the Door?

MAKING THE TRANSITION from a compartmentalized life in which I had no faith and kept everything distinctly separate to an integrated life with Christ at the center was a daunting task for me. But I am not alone.

From the early days of my faith journey until now, I have come to learn that many people wrestle with this dilemma. In addition to my role as managing partner of a national executive search firm, I am deeply involved in ministry work that offers forums for Catholic business people and professionals to gather and hear great speakers, grow in their faith, and learn about how to lead integrated lives. Much of the writing in this book reflects real-life situations of Catholics in the workplace whom I have encountered over the last few years. And not surprisingly, it is in the workplace that our faith is most commonly called into question.

Most of us spend the majority of our waking adult lives at work. The workplace today is a challenging environment in which to be open about our Christian beliefs. Political sensitivity, rigid company policies, and simple fear have led many of us to compartmentalize our faith in unhealthy and unnatural ways. I often hear people say,

"I just leave my faith at the door when I get to work." But how can one possibly separate his spiritual life from his physical body? Or better yet, how can one live a Christian life if he is daily leaving that very part of himself behind, or masked?

In the Pastoral Constitution on the Church in the Modern World (*Gaudium et Spes*), the Second Vatican Council weighed in on this particular struggle, saying that we have grown to become erroneous in our ways by creating this dichotomy between a so-called professed faith and the practice of daily life. One of the main points was to emphasize that a Christian who shirks his temporal duties does so to his neighbor, neglecting God and endangering his eternal salvation. In this declaration, they called on Christians to follow Christ's example—to be proud of the responsibility of earthly duties and to value them as religious duties, which are under God's supreme direction. What we can learn from this declaration is far more powerful than the convenience of simply "checking our faith at the door." So, how can we overcome secular obstacles to our faith and fully embrace Christ in every aspect of our day, especially at work? Simple: by integrating our faith into everything we do at work.

This does not mean we need to identify ourselves as being the "Catholic one" at work, but simply recognizing that we *are* Catholic is a good start. Yet the notion of being Catholic at work is a daunting idea for many. The thought of acting, thinking, and leading through the lens of our faith is an alien concept. In my professional life, I encounter scores of businessmen and women who have in their mind that "faith at work" means leading Bible studies in the break room over lunch or loudly evangelizing coworkers and anyone within earshot. It rarely occurs to us to think about our own faith journeys as an example we could set for others. Nor do we tend to acknowledge the Christ-inspired joy we should be radiating as the most significant and worthwhile way we can share our faith. Letting others see Jesus Christ in our lives and in our work is a powerful form of witness that will draw in others who want what we have in our lives.

If someone had told me before 2005 that I would one day write a book about integrating faith and work, I would have enjoyed a good laugh. From the time I stopped attending the Baptist Church as a teenager until I made the decision to join the Catholic Church more than two decades later, I led a very compartmentalized existence. In the early years of my career, I focused on my job and little else. After I married my wife, Sandra, and had two sons, Alex and Ryan, a few years later, I lived for both work and family, but kept those worlds distinctly separate. Faith, unfortunately, played no role in my life.

It was through the struggle (and then success) of finding my faith that I am able to openly provide tidbits of my life in this book. The pieces of the story of my unlikely journey into the Catholic Church are woven into some of the chapters of this book to provide context and to share with you my own journey of faith. When I made the life-changing decision to convert to the Catholic Church in the summer of 2005, one of the first challenges I faced was ensuring that I led a Christ-centered life that integrated faith, family, and work. I had made the sincere commitment to put Jesus Christ first in all areas of my life, and that meant my work life as well. I was faced with the challenge of ridding myself of the compartmental life I was living. In doing that, I have found that this was not just my problem, but a problem for many.

In the practice of our Catholic faith, would you agree that we are faced with a choice between a compartmentalized life or an integrated life in which faith, family, and work are unified and centered in Christ? Through sacred Scripture and Church teaching, we are asked to change our hearts, let go of our attachments to material things, and place Christ first in our lives. We are asked to let others see Jesus within us and to share our joy with others. Our humble and virtuous example to others throughout the day will positively influence their behavior and individual faith journeys. An active prayer life, one that turns our day into a conversation with God and firmly places his desires before our own, will open us up to receive boundless grace.

The reflection and discussion questions you will find at the end of each chapter are meant to stimulate thinking around the current state of your work/faith integration and how you can begin making sincere changes to enrich both aspects of your life. It is also my hope that the practical lessons and actionable ideas throughout this book and the stories of real Catholics living out their faith in the workplace will inspire you and provide the necessary tools to lead a more integrated life. It is important to remember that Catholics are meant to stand out, not blend in. Bringing your faith into the workplace is not only about fitting your life into the workplace, but also about how to integrate it wisely and effectively. Let's discover together what needs to be in your Catholic briefcase.

CHAPTER 1
Integrating Catholicism With Our Work

> *There are never really any simple answers, and there are times when it will be more of a public struggle to overcome than an inward one.*

PUTTING GOD FIRST and blending your faith with every aspect of your life will promote balance, peace, and help you on your faith journey toward a deeper relationship with God. Of course, this is easier said than done. It is a challenge, and one that takes time and effort.

Around the time of my conversion to the Church, when I was still struggling and praying about how to lead an integrated life, a friend recommended I read the writings of Blessed John Paul II. One of the first works I encountered was his apostolic exhortation *Christifideles Laici*. This passage made a great impression on me: "The unity of life of the lay faithful is of the greatest importance:

indeed they must be sanctified in everyday professional and social life. Therefore, to respond to their vocation, the lay faithful must see their daily activities as an occasion to join themselves to God, fulfill his will, serve other people and lead them to communion with God in Christ."[1] John Paul II gave words to what I had been seeking. The mission of the lay faithful forces us to consider the workplace as fertile ground in which to do God's work. As we know from numerous Scripture passages and Church teaching, we are all called to lead lives of holiness and to be witnesses for Christ. Our workplace vocation is necessarily a critical component of responding to that call. Why is this important?

Promoting this integration will help us become better Christians and reverse the negative effects—mental, emotional, moral—of keeping our faith separate from the rest of our lives. Consider this relevant perspective from my friend, frequent ministry collaborator, and mentor, Deacon Mike Bickerstaff: "We can no more stop being Catholic at work or in the public square than we can stop breathing. To do the latter is to die physically. To do the former is to die spiritually. We must resist a culture that promotes reaching for the lifestyles of the rich and famous. Jesus said that no one can serve two masters (see Matthew 6:24). The danger has been much evident in the workplace, where excessive attention to career has resulted in failed marriages and devastated families. Our jobs (careers) should support our vocations. Our vocations must never be sacrificed or neglected to support our jobs. This understanding is at the heart of integrating our faith throughout our daily lives." The challenge is to adopt new practices and strategies, not as a bunch of new "to-dos," but as part of a broader, unifying approach to balance and integration. It isn't easy, but it's worth the journey.

To help us along as we think about balance and integration, we should ask ourselves, "What are some of the real and perceived obstacles we may face to living out our faith at work? What are tangible solutions for overcoming them?" There are never really any simple answers, and there are times when it will be more of a public struggle to overcome than an inward one. Here are examples from conversations I have had with Catholic men and women over the last few years on problems they have encountered in the process of integrating faith into the workplace.

"I am afraid of losing my job if I am open about my faith at work."

This seems to be a common struggle for many professionals, with various possible solutions. For example, look carefully at your company policy on this issue….There likely won't be one. Setting a good example, sharing our joy and reflecting Christ back to others is in no way a violation of any company policy of which I am aware. There are extremes in everything, so organizing a Bible study group at work may not be the most appropriate choice. But letting others see Christ at work in you is the most fundamental and important way to be open about your faith at work.

"Authenticity, integrity, empathy, love, and other characteristics of Christianity are not valued in my company. In fact, they are discouraged."

I am often comforted and encouraged by the Apostle Paul's advice in his Letter to the Philippians: "Whatever is true, whatever is honorable, whatever is just, whatever is pure, whatever is lovely, whatever is gracious, if there is any excellence and if there is anything worthy of praise, think about these things" (Philippians 4:8).

Your faith in the workplace, your Christian values, and your practices based on those are what make you who you are. What you value most and how you choose to express that should not impinge on your work, but it can be reflected in your work ethic, your enthusiasm, and in many other ways. We need to choose whose opinion we value more highly: God's or our company's leaders'. Hiding your true Christian self is unhealthy, dangerous, and not pleasing to God. Weigh carefully the price you may be paying for submerging your beliefs (and true self) to benefit your career versus the reward you may be forfeiting in heaven.

*"I just don't have the moral courage
to be open about my faith."*

This is one of the most honest and frequently given excuses I hear. By definition, moral courage means you are willing to act on your convictions even if it costs you something, such as social acceptance or convenience. It is easy to conform to secular expectations, but difficult to publicly show your love of Jesus Christ, live out the Beatitudes, evangelize, and lead a fully integrated life. So how could we make this struggle less difficult and easier to overcome?

Perhaps if we considered the Apostle Paul's Second Letter to Timothy: "I charge you in the presence of God and of Christ Jesus, who will judge the living and the dead, and by his appearing and his kingly power: proclaim the word; be persistent whether it is convenient or inconvenient; convince, reprimand, encourage through all patience and teaching. For the time will come when people will not tolerate sound doctrine but, following their own desires and insatiable curiosity, will accumulate teachers and will stop listening to the truth and will be diverted to myths. But you, be self-possessed in all circumstances; put up with hardship; perform the work of an evangelist; fulfill your ministry" (2 Timothy 4:1–5). Paul teaches us how to be courageous in this letter. Through persistence and dedication to our faith, we will overcome the diversions that keep us from being faithful in the workplace.

"I love Christ and his Church, but I don't always know the appropriate thing to say about my faith, especially at work."

Ponder the advice that has been attributed to Saint Francis of Assisi, "Preach the Gospel at all times. Use words if necessary."[2] Don't worry about being "good enough." We are all sinners and fall short of the glory of God. It is the love and charity we give others and our daily example of Christ's love within us that show others we are Christians. Our daily deeds will reflect our true Christian faith. If we are acting as lights for Christ, people will be drawn to us, and the Holy Spirit will work through us. If necessary, the words will come.

"I am not comfortable sharing anything personal, especially about my faith."

This is also a very common challenge. The first step is to acknowledge that forging a meaningful and authentic connection with someone will require a degree of "opening up." Making your conversations all about business is, well, boring. One of the easiest ways I have found to overcome this obstacle is to humbly share my own background, including my faith story. I don't mention faith in every conversation, but mentioning that I am a Catholic convert usually generates a lot of questions from the other person, providing an opportunity to open up and share my faith. Pick your spots, but humble and honest sharing on your part will likely be well-received. And remember that our personal witness to others may provide them the inspiration and motivation to embrace faith.

Those are just a few examples of the many that are encountered day in and day out. So how can we overcome these obstacles and lead a more integrated life? It must be more than just an idea. It should permeate every aspect of your life. Put God first in all things and let his will become your will. And remember Paul's letter: Consistency, not arbitrary experimentation, is the key to success. And remember that action—faithful action—is at the root of your faith and will lead to a faithful workplace integration.

Here are five actionable ideas that may help you integrate your Catholic faith with your work:

1. Pray. We will not succeed in this effort without a prayerful life. Say a daily rosary, pray before the Blessed Sacrament during eucharistic adoration, pray in the morning, pray throughout the day, pray with your kids, and offer up your burdens to the Lord in prayer… just pray (see Appendix 5). Remember the motto of the Benedictine Order: "To work is to pray."[3]

2. See Christ in others and make sure they see Christ at work in you. Look at your coworkers and clients differently. See Christ in each of them and make sure you reflect the joy of Christ back to them.

3. Join or start a ministry that promotes this effort. Look around your parish for ministries that might help in your effort to integrate or start one with the blessing of your pastor. I have led the business association ministry in my parish for years, where we bring professionals together in the parish (and from surrounding parishes) each month to hear local speakers from the business and professional community discuss their faith journeys. With the right structure and format, it can be the catalyst for encouraging integration on a large scale. See Appendix 4 for a road map on how to build a Catholic Business Group.

4. Know our faith. It is easier to embrace our faith in the public square and at work when we better understand our faith. One of the underlying causes of the obstacles listed earlier is the fear that we will not be able to explain or defend our Catholicism to others. We should never stop being students, especially of our faith. We should immerse ourselves in Scripture, the catechism, the Church Fathers, the lives of the Saints, etc. This is an important part of our duty as faithful Catholics. (There is much wisdom to be found in two incredible documents: John Paul II's *Christifideles Laici* and Vatican II's Pastoral Constitution on the Church in the Modern World (*Gaudium et Spes*). See Appendix 1.)

5. Surrender and put God's will before our own. This is the most challenging, yet the most rewarding and most necessary action. If we are humble and God is truly first, everything else will fall into place and integration will occur naturally. Consider Saint Augustine's famous motto: "Love [God] and [then] do what you will."[4] In other words, if you love God and his will, then doing "what you will" will, in fact, be doing what God wills.

Integrating your Christian life into your work life is not a cure-all for every challenge you will face as a Catholic in the workplace. I can only share with you my experience and the experiences of the men and women I know whose lives have been positively affected by this effort. But by doing so, it is my hope and belief that Catholic business people and professionals will see a dramatic change in their lives if they embrace this idea.

The key to this change is in recognizing that Christ should never compete for our time. Living our busy lives and putting him first are NOT mutually exclusive. In fact, it should not even be possible. Jesus is not to be considered an addition to our lives. He is the reason for our lives. As Deacon Mike mentioned earlier, integrating our Christian faith does not mean that we include our faith in a to-do list at work. Instead of viewing the daily practice of our faith as adding more time to already-packed schedules, we need to integrate our lives with Christ at the center of everything we do. Patrick Lencioni said it best in his foreword to this book: "I am not going to get my faith life squared away personally until I make it the center of my life in every way, including at work. I can no more justify keeping my faith out of my job than I can my marriage, my family, or my Sunday Mass."

Consider for a moment what would happen if the millions of Catholics in this country became more integrated and showed more active faith in the workplace, and through acts of selfless love, the guidance of the Holy Spirit, and the Church's teaching began to positively change their actions and inspire others to do good. We would permanently change the world.

REFLECTION AND DISCUSSION

- Do I consider the workplace "fertile ground to do God's work?" Why? Why not?
- Reflect on what I may be doing today to live out my Catholic faith at work. What is working? What can be improved?
- Do the obstacles to integrating faith and work shared by other Catholics in this chapter resonate with me? Would I add others? Make a list for later reflection and discussion.
- Does Christ compete for my time? Reflect on how to make him the center of my life and not simply an addition to an already busy day.

CHAPTER 2

Finding Strength
in Surrender

> *And when you find yourself making*
> *excuses, becoming afraid to let go, or are*
> *even trying to maintain control over your*
> *life, keep your thoughts and focus on how*
> *you can best serve Christ.*

SURRENDER, giving control of our lives to Christ, is an enormous obstacle to living out our faith in the workplace, or anyplace for that matter. Surrendering to Christ and putting his will before my own for the first time more than five years ago was the very moment I felt stronger than at any other time in my life. By surrendering, the strength of the Lord flowed through me, energized me, gave me courage, and put me on the path to a life of discipleship filled with meaning. The recognition that I had to give up control and experience the death of my old self allowed me to put absolute trust in him; without which, my soul's conversion would not have been possible. Even more important, I have come to recognize that my surrender and conversion is an ongoing process and not a one-time event. It is through daily surrender that we can develop trust in him and in ourselves as we grow in faith in the workplace.

Yet, so many good people I encounter each day struggle with this idea of surrender. It is almost as if we have developed barriers around our hearts that keep the world at an emotional distance. The most important casualty, however, is our relationship with Christ, as we often wind up keeping him at a distance as well. I observe men and women every day who come right up against a deeper faith and a closer relationship with Jesus, only to walk away. Why? After countless conversations with a large number of my brothers and sisters in Christ, it comes down to three main obstacles in the way of our trustful surrender to the Lord: pride, fear, and excuses. Do any of these obstacles resonate with you? At various times, they have all clicked with me. When our pride gets hold of us, we forget our roles outside of the workplace: as a spouse, parent, or friend. When fear controls our faith, we fail to submit to Christ and his divine will. And in making excuses, we create barriers between God and us. In order to avoid these obstacles, therefore, it's important to know how and when to surrender.

When we are experiencing success in business and our personal lives are flourishing, do we think about putting the Lord first in our lives? Is submitting to his will top of mind? Do we thank him? Before answering these questions, consider another perspective, following the words of Saint John Eudes: "You can advance farther in grace in one hour during a time of affliction than in many days during a time of consolation." How do we view Jesus when times are tough? We may have lost our job or be going through serious financial problems. Maybe our children are struggling with peer pressure at school or a family member is dying. How would we view Jesus then? When is our trust in him most apparent?

In my professional life, I encounter dozens of people each month who are going through career transition, especially in this difficult economy (see Appendix 3). Many have shared with me that they have turned to our Lord for help in these tough times when they were at their weakest moments. They turn to him when they used to rely only on themselves. The point I am making is we often turn to Jesus when we are in crisis and ask him for help and strength. Crisis can be a helpful catalyst to truly and unreservedly surrender to his will, and any means to achieve that end is worthwhile. But we should not wait until our backs are against the wall to pray the words, "I am no longer in charge Jesus, please lead me."

To give ourselves daily to Jesus Christ, it is important to put our absolute trust in him. What have we got to lose? When I think about my own faith, I remember what Pope Benedict XVI said: "If we let Christ into our lives, we lose nothing, nothing, absolutely nothing of what makes life free, beautiful, and great. No! Only in this friendship are the doors of life opened wide. Only in this friendship is the great potential of human existence truly revealed." When we give ourselves up, God lets himself in. And that is exactly what he did for me.

In the second Mass I ever attended (in October 2005, shortly after my wife and I made the decision to join the Catholic Church), I went through a powerful personal conversion. I was trembling, sweating, nervous, and felt weak at the beginning of the Mass. My family thought I was having a heart attack! This strange feeling lasted for about ten minutes. What happened in those few precious minutes was life-altering. I went into the church that morning feeling lost. I knew I needed help and that I no longer had the answers. I remember praying silently to God to lead me and acknowledging I was no longer in charge. I felt so weak because I had never asked God for anything before, and I didn't know how to relinquish control. When I prayed those words, gave up control, and sincerely surrendered to his will, I felt a surge of strength and a sense of peace that felt like a wind blowing right through me. I had given up more than twenty years of stubbornness, ego, and pride that had been accumulating since I last attended the Baptist Church as a teenager. When I humbly surrendered to his will, the Lord gave me strength and a sense of peace I still feel to this day. I still struggle with placing Christ first in every aspect of my life, and I have problems like everyone else. But knowing that he will forgive me, love me, guide me, and bless me keeps me coming back again and again to the place where I pray the words, "I surrender Lord, please lead me."

Your experience may be quite different from mine. But recognizing those obstacles that stand in your way is the first step toward a stronger faith in the workplace. One of the key obstacles to surrendering is pride. All of us have this in abundance. The good news is there is a cure: humility. The virtue of humility is the best way to counter the sin of pride. Best-selling Catholic author Dr. Peter Kreeft wrote, "Pride does not mean an exaggerated opinion of your own worth; that is vanity. Pride means playing God, demanding to be God. 'Better to reign in hell than serve in heaven,' says Satan, justifying his rebellion in Milton's *Paradise Lost*. That is the formula for pride. Pride is the total 'my will be done.' Humility is 'thy will be done.' Humility is focused on God, not self. Humility is not an exaggeratedly low opinion of yourself. Humility is self-forgetfulness. A humble man never tells you how bad he is. He's too busy thinking about you to talk about himself."[5] How do you recognize pride? Or better yet, how do you surrender to it? Consider these points:

- Do your pride and ego always get in the way of work relationships? What about personal ones?
- Do you ever ask, "How will my friends, peers, and work colleagues judge me?"
- Do you feel, "It is tough to be vulnerable?"

Most of the time, these moments of pride are what keep us from surrendering to God on a daily basis and eventually make us fearful of that surrender.[6] I remember very well what my life was like before surrendering to the Lord and putting him first. All I had was family and work, and I was in charge (I thought) of my own destiny. I dealt with life's challenges as they came and pridefully took the credit when things went well. I thought I was the strong husband and father my own father had been. I thought I was in control. But God had other plans for me, and I know I am not alone. Most of us are afraid to surrender, and eventually this fear becomes another obstacle to face, in addition to pride.

Fear constantly keeps us from daily surrender, and most often it stems from our pride and ego. I knew that if I didn't let go of my pride, I would not have God in my life. And I knew I needed to learn humility. But I was afraid. I wanted to keep control. When considering the previous points on pride, did you feel any of these:

- Fear of giving up control/not being in charge?
- Fear that the cost of surrender will be too great?
- Fear of losing personal freedom?

More often than not, fear is perceived as a loss; and rather than losing, we try to gain more control. But isn't it tough to go it alone? Seriously, how effective are we if we rely only on ourselves for the answers? I don't know about you, but I tried that way for more than two decades, and it was very difficult. Now that I live a life in which

Christ is in charge, and after having seen the other side, I pray that I never have to fly solo again. But doing that not only means giving up my pride and fear—I need to stop making excuses.

Excuses separate us from receiving all of God's love day to day. Often in our busy lives, we refuse to admit the obstacles that keep us from surrendering to God and in return come up with excuses like the following:

- There is an emotional barrier around the heart, formed at a young age, to keep people at a distance (which is my personal experience).
- "I was raised to keep this stuff inside, like my dad."
- "Work and family stress is hard enough. I don't have time for this right now."
- "I go to Mass every Sunday. Isn't that enough?"

The choice to surrender to Christ and place him first takes commitment, and the journey to get there is difficult. I know a lot of good, smart people who have been deeply moved by an emotional meeting/weekend, inspirational book or personal tragedy to make this commitment, only to lapse back into "me first" behaviors weeks later. It can happen to anyone. This commitment has to be firm and will require persistence, courage, and sacrifice. And when you find yourself making excuses, becoming afraid to let go, or are even trying to maintain control over your life, keep your thoughts and focus on how you can best serve Christ.

Please consider your answers (as I have many times) to these important questions:

- Do I want to be a better spouse?
- Do I want to be a better parent?
- Do I desire a stronger faith journey in the Catholic Church?
- Do I want to be a better son or daughter to my parents?
- Do I want to be a better friend?
- Can I be more involved in the community and helping others?
- Do I want to be a better leader at work?

As we ponder these questions, it is probably safe to assume we said "yes" to each one. Now, think about surrendering yourself to Jesus and asking him for help. We know what it is like to go it alone, and if we are honest with ourselves, the results are not that great.

Surrendering to him, letting our old self go, and placing him first will change everything. We will receive from Christ his grace, guidance, and love which, in turn, will positively affect our relationships with our spouses, children, friends, and coworkers. We will see our faith journeys catch fire as we begin to appreciate the truth and beauty of our Catholic faith. We will be perceived differently as people begin to see Christ at work in us. But consider this: Jesus Christ died on the cross for us. He redeemed our sins. He loves us unconditionally. The only way to heaven is through him. What does he want in return? He simply asks for ALL of us—mind, body, and soul. He wants us to place him first in our lives, before family, friends, work…everything. Think about the list of questions we just answered and place "Christ-inspired" in front of father or mother, husband or wife, son or daughter, friend, leader, etc. How can this not be desirable?

As you consider the substance of this chapter and how it speaks to you, please be mindful that you can't simply "add Jesus to your life" and share control with him. He requires all of us, all the time. In return for our trustful surrender, he will fill us with his strength, his love, his peace and shape us into the spouses, parents, friends, leaders, and Catholics we always wanted to be. With his strength within us, we will find ourselves often giving to others and sharing our newfound selfless love with the people in our lives. Please ask yourselves: What do we really lose by surrendering to Christ? Then, ask: What do I lose by failing to surrender to Christ?

I would like to share a wonderful and relevant prayer by Saint Ignatius of Loyola called the Suscipe:

> Take, Lord, and receive all my liberty,
> my memory, my understanding
> and my entire will,
> All I have and call my own.
> You have given all to me.
> To you, Lord, I return it.
> Everything is yours; do with it what you will.
> Give me only your love and your grace.
> That is enough for me.[7]

As we ponder the idea of living out our faith in the workplace, remember it all begins with a daily surrender that will require the virtues of trust, courage, and persistence. Anything less than total surrender to our Lord will doom our efforts at an integrated life to failure. We must trust that in return for our trustful surrender, Jesus will provide us with the strength we need to be successful in business and life and overcome the obstacles of pride, fear, and excuses. Finally, we must place our trust in God.

Let's remember to pray for one another, that we will achieve what Saint Paul wrote: "Yet I live, no longer I, but Christ lives in me" (Galatians 2:20).

REFLECTION AND DISCUSSION

- Reflect for a moment on the idea of surrender. Is this easy or difficult for me? Do the obstacles shared to surrendering resonate with me?
- Consider times in my life when I have faced crisis. How did I overcome the challenge(s)? Did I turn to our Lord for help?
- How did I answer the questions in the last section? Reflect on how the answers might affect my actions going forward.

CHAPTER 3

Time to Think

*We are addicted to background "noise"
and connecting with others through our
computers and smartphones.*

AS BUSY PROFESSIONALS with compounding responsibilities, isn't it becoming more and more difficult to find time just to think? Commiserating with colleagues and friends, we share how our workdays are filled with an almost obsessed focus on getting as much work done as possible, countless meetings and squeezing every bit of air out of our schedules. In our other roles as fathers/mothers and husbands/wives, we're faced with another harried stretch of time each evening filled with family dinner, kids' activities, and the myriad other things that families require. If you are called to the single life, quality time with loved ones and friends also is a challenge. Weekends are often just as hectic.

Clever vernacular such as "perpetual hurry syndrome" and "time poverty" are beginning to circulate when describing this phenomenon, but I simply choose to call it alarming. We make decisions all day long, but how much of it is reactive and responding to what others throw your way? Taking time to pray, think strategically, be creative or even pause to reflect on an issue before responding is a growing challenge. The fact that many of us view time to think, pray, and reflect as a luxury is a sad indictment of the culture in which we live.

Thus, we are addicted to background "noise" and connecting with others through our computers and smartphones. I'm not opposed to technology, but recognize how I've allowed it to exacerbate my challenge with finding quiet time. What used to be a leisurely drive to work a decade ago is now crammed with phone calls. Waiting for appointments to arrive, stops at red lights, and elevator rides are now opportunities to respond with my iPhone to the barrage of e-mails I receive daily. In an effort to become more efficient, I am sacrificing thinking time in an unhealthy way. Do you face similar struggles?

While writing this chapter, I contacted Dr. Paul Voss, a Catholic husband, father, gifted national speaker, author, and president of Ethikos. His company provides leadership and business ethics consulting for companies all over the country. He is also an associate professor of literature at Georgia State University. Dr. Voss is a busy man who integrates his Catholic faith into his daily work life and values his quiet time for prayer and reflection. I spoke with him about the challenge of finding quality time:

Q. Dr. Voss, how would you describe the challenges with work/life balance in your client's organizations?

A. Finding the proper balance between work and life is something of a current preoccupation, with scores of books and self-help guides willing to assist with the process. In fact, we have a term—

workaholics—for those who place work and the quest for material advantage above other aspects of life in an unhealthy and even addictive fashion. The pressure for profit and productivity—especially in trying economic times—exacerbates this situation. Many of my corporate clients cite this as the number-one challenge they face when trying to create productive, healthy cultures.

Q. Is this a relatively recent challenge in the workplace?

A. Modern life did not create this problem of work-life balance. In fact, the tension between the life of the mind/reflection (*otium*) and the life of work/activity (*negotium*) dates back to antiquity. The Romans, for example, placed great emphasis upon military achievement and conquest (*negotium*), but they also tried to cultivate a life of beauty and philosophy (*otium*). The early Christians dedicated an entire day to leisure and abstinence from work—Sunday, the first day of the week, in honor of Christ's resurrection. Daily prayers, especially the Angelus, and the frequent "hearing of Mass" allowed medieval and Renaissance Christians to fully integrate work and faith.

Q. How do you suggest the modern professional find peace and time for reflection in today's busy world?

A. Today the expression of faith and the cultivation of an interior, philosophical life, is largely confined to Sunday morning (certainly not the entire day). We have portioned off less and less time for reading, prayer, reflection, examination, and leisure. We seem to have lost the rhythm of the Renaissance world. Early in the twentieth century, T.S. Eliot could openly desire the "still point in a turning world," a time and space for reflection and contemplation. It was hard—even in the 1930s—to find such a space that one needed the desire to find the harmony. Today, perhaps the greatest threat is a lost vocabulary itself and the subsequent loss of even the desire to cultivate a life of the mind and tranquility of soul—on being in the world but not of the world. It's a struggle, a heroic struggle indeed. But if we fail to even try, we lose part of our humanity.

Do Dr. Voss' insights resonate with you? Is our work/life balance dramatically out of kilter because we are not pursuing those things that matter most in life? Has the technological age, which was supposed to result in a time of increased leisure, in fact, enslaved us? As you ponder these questions, think about the time you spend with these technologies versus the time you spend thinking and pondering your work/daily activities.

Time to think, time to pray, time with family, time with friends—these are the components of the fuller and richer lives we all want to lead. Work will always demand as much of our time as we allow. But is technology the real culprit? Probably not. We have the freedom to choose how we spend our time and should take this responsibility onto ourselves. Remember that technology was intended to serve us and not the other way around.

So how do we create these respites of time we so desperately need? It's the little things, the small steps that will help us find our quiet reflection time. Here are some ideas:

1. Start your day on a different note.

Don't run to your computer and turn it on. Rather than checking e-mail or reading the overnight news the moment you wake up, designate the first thirty minutes for reflection, reading, and prayer. Have a cup of coffee, sit down, and think about your day. Or perhaps reading or exercise stimulates your brain. Whatever it is, make it your time—it's the one part of the day when clients aren't calling and nobody is making demands on your schedule.

Set this time aside for God, then yourself. We will likely exercise the greatest control of our personal lives by allowing this time to be ours and ours with God.

2. Put it on your calendar.

You know the saying that "if it isn't scheduled, it will never happen?" Try blocking out small windows of time each day for prayer and reflection. I borrowed an idea from the Jesuits called the Daily Examen, which I mention a few times in this book (see Appendix 2). I schedule five-minute blocks of time throughout the day to pray, reflect on my actions, and think about the future. Schedule these time blocks around travel, meals, and bedtimes. As I mentioned before about integrating, scheduling time for various activities will help to create a balance in your faith life. Want to ensure that you are home for dinner each night? Put it on your calendar and schedule around it. The same thing goes for important events in the lives of your family members. Make your work life conform to what is truly important, not the other way around.

3. Introduce simplicity into your life.

Try turning your iPhone or BlackBerry off once in a while, especially when you are around your family and friends. Try reading a book instead of listening to the audio version. Spend time with good friends who will challenge you. Listen to beautiful music or watch a classic movie. Take a long walk with your spouse or significant other. Do something outside with your family every day. Volunteer to serve those who are not as fortunate as you. Get some time for yourself on the weekend and make sure your spouse does as well. Downsize your possessions, buy a smaller house, live more simply, and get rid of what you don't need. Remember, you really can't take it with you.

4. Don't feed your compulsions.

As a practical measure, turn off the "ding" when new e-mail arrives. It can wait. Don't feel compelled to answer immediately. Do the same on your smartphone. Turning off the audio or LED notification and checking for e-mails at the appropriate time can add to your current focus and minimizes those distractions that prevent us from being a part of a more fully integrated life. Look at other tendencies that negatively affect your thinking time and make some simple changes.

5. Hold mini-retreats every quarter.

Take a day off once a quarter, if not more frequently. Use this time only to relax and plan. Explain to your loved ones that you need this to collect yourself and get reenergized. Check into a hotel overnight. Or even better, find a Catholic retreat center near you. The toughest challenge with a mini-retreat is to leave your phone and computer behind, so try journaling instead. You owe it to yourself, your teammates, and your company to recharge your batteries and think more strategically in a quiet place.

6. Spend time with people who will challenge you and make you think.

It can be as formal as inviting your team to a meeting where you throw a problem on the white board for discussion, or as casual as inviting a few friends to lunch to debate politics. When in the presence of your team, colleagues, or friends, ask thought-provoking questions. In an effort to break free from simply sharing regurgitated ideas and information, ask "why" more often. Go to coffee or lunch with friends who will help you grow in your Catholic faith. Regardless of how you do it, this open debate and discussion is healthy and will feed and stimulate you in important ways.

7. Designate certain windows of time as "gadget free."

Choose times in the day (car rides are ideal) when all electronics are turned off, even the radio. This will take discipline, but imagine the car as your safe haven and "thought incubator." During a recent Lenten season, I gave up radio and TV, and it helped me reclaim some glorious quiet time in my car and at home. I regained my reflection time, prayed more, did more spiritual reading, and brought some balance back in my life.

This last point has made a tremendous impact on my life, and on my journey toward conversion into the Church. Around the time of my conversion, a good friend gave me a beautiful leather writing journal. That thoughtful gift quickly prompted much alteration in my daily routine that I still practice today. I enjoy writing and often used to e-mail myself article ideas or leave myself messages at work about writing topics—adding to the volumes of messages I already received. Now, I take the journal with me everywhere and find I'm reaching for it instead of my technology enablers. Writing by hand provides me a few precious moments between appointments or in the early hours of the day to gather my thoughts on a number of topics, and the process has been rejuvenating.

In the end, our faith journeys rely on moments during the day when we are able to pull away and to just be one with God. By taking these few precious moments to reflect and to think, we are able to strengthen our faith in God that reflects back on others. As many people have a tendency to do at some point in their lives (I am, for example), take stock of what's important. I am determined to find the time I need for God, family, work, and me. We give the important areas of our lives our best effort when we're calm, rested, and thoughtful. We own the responsibility to make the necessary changes to give ourselves what we need. What part of your schedule will you reclaim today to have prayer, reflection, and thinking time?

REFLECTION AND DISCUSSION

- Do you feel there is never enough time to get everything done in your day? Reflect on what is important, but currently missing, and how you can integrate these elements into your day.
- Does your day control you or do you control your day? How can you curb the onslaught of noise, information, demands on your schedule, and conflicting priorities to find time for God, your family, friends, and yourself?
- What additional ideas would you add to the list of ideas on regaining quiet time for reflection and prayer? Make a list for yourself for future review and reflection.

CHAPTER 4

Making Time for Prayer

> *We rarely stop to consider the harm we are doing ourselves by ignoring our need for peace and quiet.*

HOW OFTEN does it occur to us to make our prayer lives a priority? Do we even know how to get started? How about if we stop making prayer conform to our day and instead make the day conform to our prayer lives. Not that this is easily done all the time, but it will help to start us off on the right path toward becoming more faithful Christians at work.

When I think of people who excel at integrating prayer with the busy workday, one of the best examples I can think of is Jennifer Baugh. Jennifer impressed me the first time she contacted me more than a year ago via a business networking Web site. She was starting a Dallas-based networking group for Catholics in their 20s and 30s called Young Catholic Professionals and wanted to discuss my experiences with similar groups I have started in Atlanta. Jennifer has an impressive background, and I love her passion for encouraging a culture of Catholic community in all aspects of our lives, especially in the workplace.

In one of our discussions, I asked Jennifer how she makes time for prayer during her hectic days. She told me she has long been inspired by one of her favorite verses in Scripture, "Be still and know that I am God" (Psalm 46:11)! It is how Jennifer makes prayer the backbone of her day. She says: "As a young professional, there are constant pressures to perform and exceed expectations in a new working environment. I often felt that as a recent MBA graduate working for a high-intensity consulting firm that I had a great responsibility to react to every challenge with complete calm and confidence. The temptation to lose my spiritual center amidst the demands of the corporate world was real. My BlackBerry never left my side as I awaited each e-mail with anxiety and disquiet.

"By the grace of God, my office building was located right next to the downtown Cathedral where daily Mass was celebrated at noon. Each day I would look forward to leaving the office for this time of prayer and reflection. Seeing the other men and women who were taking time out of their busy schedules to participate in the Mass was a powerful and humbling experience. Together we listened to the eucharistic prayer that says, 'In your mercy keep us free from sin and protect us from all anxiety.'

"Making time for prayer has helped me find balance to my work and reminded me not to be so inwardly focused on my trials. As Saint Paul tells us, 'Have no anxiety at all, but in everything, by prayer and petition, with thanksgiving, make your requests known to God' (Philippians 4:6). Prayer is our great weapon and will help us weather any storm in our professional and personal lives. Making time for prayer will also enable us to act in a Christian manner in business decision-making rather than react emotionally to new situations."

Jennifer is eminently practical and very disciplined. She sets aside time for prayer when she wakes up and before she goes to bed, but finds that going to daily Mass as often as possible provides the best opportunity for prayer. She is also fond of prayer in the car and leaves her rosary beads hanging from her mirror to remind her to use the time for thanksgiving and reflection. Jennifer finds that using her daily routines to help her stay close to Christ is rewarding and helpful. Lest you think her prayer is always scheduled, Jennifer is working on being more spontaneous in her prayer life. She shared with me that, "Life is full of contradictions. I am working on praying throughout the day as the Spirit moves me. There are so many opportunities to thank God or to offer up a struggle. My favorite prayer is the Memorare, which I tend to pray when I am worried about something. I also have started to pray the Jesus prayer when I am pressed for time."

Thinking about Jennifer, what can you learn from her and perhaps integrate into your own daily prayers? Knowing that we are all different in our spiritual and prayer lives, I encourage you to take from Jennifer's experience the values that it might have in your own workplace. It is a challenge, but it will also strengthen your workplace faith.

In the last chapter, we explored the difficulties that we, as busy professionals, have finding quiet time for prayer, reflection, and thinking. That, in addition to finding time to prayer, are the biggest challenges I most frequently hear from business and professional people. In today's world, the trend is toward squeezing the air out of our schedules and being more productive. We rarely stop to consider the harm we are doing ourselves by ignoring our need for peace and quiet. By just taking the time to think and pray each day, it will become easier and easier to work and to share our faith in the workplace.

For me, the difficulty in finding the time to think and pray came in those moments when my faith was new; when I still relied on books to find faith, not prayer. Before I began my RCIA classes in the summer of 2006, I studied the Catholic faith in earnest. I tend to intellectualize everything, and my first thoughts were to learn everything I could about our faith. I quickly realized there was more to Catholicism than knowledge, history, and tradition. I then began to focus on being the best Catholic I could be and started on my true faith journey, versus simply immersing myself in books. One of the biggest obstacles for me in those days was my lack of prayer life. I knew I needed to pray, but I couldn't ever remember sincerely praying about anything. I was struggling with the typical male challenge of asking for help, especially asking God for help. Who was I to bother him with my petty problems?

I finally sought guidance. I shared my prayer challenges with one of our deacons and asked for advice. He looked at me with some amusement and said I was approaching prayer the wrong way. "Don't worry about asking for help just yet," he said. He advised me to simply praise God for who he is, and then thank him for what he has done...praise first, then thanksgiving. Eventually, I learned to ask God for help and guidance, but my real prayer life started by praising and then offering thanks to him. I finally got it. I understood that my faith would never grow unless I had an active prayer life. This was the beginning of my prayer journey that has continued to unfold and grow with each passing day. I would like to share with you the stages of my prayer journey as a Catholic, lessons I have learned and insights into how I pray in hopes you will find my experiences helpful.

STAGE ONE of my prayer life was learning to thank God and be grateful. Going to him in prayer every day and reflecting on the blessings and burdens in my life are how I learned to appreciate and acknowledge the Lord's role in my life. I never start a prayer without thanking him. I have also learned to recognize his role in my work life, and I frequently go to him in prayer before major decisions and when I need support.

STAGE TWO for me was learning to ask for forgiveness. I go to reconciliation frequently, but it is still important for me to ask the Lord for his pardon and forgiveness when I commit a sin, which is more frequently than I care to admit. It has become a daily examination of conscience for me to reflect on where I have failed him and ask for forgiveness and the grace to not commit that sin again. This reflection time is easily incorporated into the Daily Examen that I have mentioned in this book (see Appendix 2). I often take moments out of my day to think back on where I may have wronged him, or perhaps acted in self-interest. Doing this daily, I am able to move forward in forgiveness.

STAGE THREE was asking for his help and guidance. This stage of prayer is also when I learned to pray for others and their needs. Help is the key here. I think men in general struggle with asking for help, and I am no exception. My growing prayer life and deepening faith journey have given me the humility to realize I don't have all the answers and that Jesus absolutely wants to help me. Early on I would tentatively ask for help with the big stuff such as getting my family into heaven, blessing our priests and deacons, blessing my business, and so on. Now, I am very comfortable asking for his help and guidance in every facet of my life. But first I had to gain the humility to recognize that without our Lord, I am nothing, and I need his strength. Asking for help in my work life was once a major struggle for me, but as I shed my old compartmentalized existence for an integrated life, I recognized where I needed perhaps the most help was at work.

STAGE FOUR in my prayer journey has been learning to completely unburden myself to the Lord. This has occurred only in the past few years. I have always been inclined to carry my stress, frustrations, worries and fears like a secret weight around my neck. As I got better at asking the Lord for help, I began asking him to help lighten these mental and emotional burdens. I am so grateful that I now can go to him and absolutely give up to him whatever is weighing me down, from work stress to concern about my children's futures. Whatever it is, I share it with Jesus as he asked us to: "Come to me, all you who labor and are burdened, and I will give you rest. Take my yoke upon you and learn from me, for I am meek and humble of heart; and you will find rest for your selves. For my yoke is easy and my burden light" (Matthew 11:28–30).

I am confident there will be more and evolving stages of prayer growth for me if I am humble and focused on deepening my relationship with Christ. Saint Teresa of Avila wrote frequently on the stages of prayer, especially in her book *The Interior Castle*. I hope to reach the contemplative and mystical prayer life she describes in her works, and pray that Jesus will lead me there. But I have a lot yet to learn.

Now I'd like to share some important, big-picture lessons I have learned in my prayer life:

1. Make time for prayer; just do it!

As I stated earlier, if you don't schedule prayer time and stick to it, it will not happen. And again, I encourage you to include prayer time on your calendar. You should start your day with prayer and continue to pray throughout the day. Set aside short blocks of time. Making time for prayer is like making time for your family. How much time are you willing to spend a day with your loved ones? It should not be a struggle to commit a small amount of time each day to pray. How you do it, or for how long, is not nearly as important as the act of doing it.

2. Block out the noise.

Turn off the car radio, watch less or no TV, reduce unnecessary computer time, and seek out more quiet moments during the day. Take a walk by yourself at lunch to clear the cobwebs. Turn off your cell phone on the way home and use that time for quiet reflection. Because our jobs typically demand it, it is difficult to pray and hear God when we are distracted by the noise of the world. It is easy to schedule around it, if you must, but remember: It's not another "to-do" list item.

3. Have the proper disposition.

It is important to have the right attitude of humility and trust that God can and will help us before we start praying. Reading Scripture or a book of meditations such as *In Conversation With God* or *Imitation of Christ* every day before prayer will help prepare our minds and hearts to approach the Lord in a deeper and more meaningful way. We should always end our prayers feeling grateful for the blessings God has given us in our lives.

4. Work through the "dry patches."

We all experience dryness in our prayers or have trouble focusing. We may feel that God is not listening. We may fall into the trap of asking God to validate what we want, instead of submitting to his will. I am certain that we will all likely experience this, but keep at it. We may realize that our dry patches come as a result of rushing prayer or going through the motions, which we should always avoid. In those cases, we have to revert back to taking the time to think and be alone with God; that will lead back to a prayerful life.

5. Practice more listening and less talking.

As our work schedules continuously fill up, we often become so busy talking and working that we don't hear him. That detracts from our quality prayer time. I have a tendency to ask God to grant my requests when I should be focused on asking him what he requires of me. It is easy to fall into cycles of "I'm too busy" or to simply forget to take prayer time. Don't let your work become so busy that you forget your role in God's plan.

6. Realize we can't grow in our faith journeys without growing our prayer lives.

We simply will not grow our relationship with Christ unless we do so through prayer. According to the *Catechism of the Catholic Church* (2744): "Prayer is a vital necessity. Proof from the contrary is no less convincing: if we do not allow the Spirit to lead us, we fall back into the slavery of sin."[8] Make time for prayer throughout the workday, and you will find a more peaceful and enjoyable work environment.

Finally, I would like to share insights on how I pray and what led me to where I am now, in hopes that they will inspire and help you deepen your own prayer life:

I get up early each morning and start every day by reading Scripture in the quiet of my home. I then read and reflect on various meditations and how they apply to my life. I follow with the Morning Offering, praying for the special intentions of friends and loved ones, and then finish with the Angelus, which is traditionally prayed three times a day (at 6 a.m., noon, and 6 p.m.)

I started praying the rosary a few years ago and typically pray it on my way to work or during my infrequent visits to the treadmill. I put off praying the rosary for a long time, but it is becoming a critical part of my prayer life and is a true blessing. This goes hand-in-hand with my ever-deepening love and appreciation for our Blessed Mother and asking for her intercession and help.

The Daily Examen, developed by the Jesuits, is a critical part of my daily routine (see Appendix 2). Basically we are asked to stop five times throughout the day for a few minutes of reflection and prayer. Each stopping point has a specific purpose, such as the prayer of thanksgiving, prayer for insight, prayer to find God in all things that day, prayer for your desires and what you seek from God, and finally a prayer about the future and what you will resolve to do tomorrow. It is best to put these five-minute blocks on your calendar throughout the day so you will be reminded.

If it is not on my calendar, it rarely happens. I schedule different prayers at various times in the day on my iPhone. This helps me remember to pray, forces me to make time for it and allows me to read the prayer if I have not yet memorized it. This is a good way to integrate our faith with technology.

In a nod to the incredible advances in technology, I will share that I find a number of Catholic apps for my iPhone to be very helpful for integrating my faith into my busy workday (see Helpful Resources in Appendix 1). BlackBerry, Android and other smartphones may have similar products worth investigating.

Pray at every meal, public and private, regardless of your companions. It is important for us be thankful, acknowledge Christ, and ask for his blessing.

My wife and I pray with our children every night. It is important for them to develop their own prayer lives, but they need to see our example, and we also grow by sharing our prayer lives with them.

I have been a eucharistic adoration guardian since January 2007, and this is the best hour of my week (see Appendix 5). No matter what is happening in my life, I can come into the Real Presence of Christ and open up to him in prayer. It is uplifting, energizing, and a great way to start my day. I also stop by our parish chapel to pray before or after work as often as I can.

I certainly don't have all the answers on prayer. I simply want to share with you as someone who struggles with the same issues and obstacles as you that my prayer life and my faith journey have grown together. I presented you with many ideas and suggestions, but remember that they are yours to accommodate into your own life. Start at a comfortable place and work until you reach your level of comfort. The important thing is that you just do it. The most significant changes in my prayer life occurred when I made the commitment to "just do it" and started scheduling my prayer time on my computer and iPhone.

I didn't have any kind of prayer life before converting to the Catholic Church, and now I couldn't imagine life without it. To me, prayer is any time that I turn my attention to God and away from myself alone. It can be accomplished in a variety of ways. Feeling worthy or inspired is not a great barometer for measuring our prayer lives. Praying for the desire for prayer is worthwhile and a good start. My life, especially my work life, is richer and more fulfilling because my days are now built on a foundation of prayer.

REFLECTION AND DISCUSSION

- Think for a minute about how I am praying during the day. Is it an add-on to my already busy schedule? Is there time set aside for prayer? What will I sacrifice to gain more prayer time?
- Reflect on the self-discipline and devotion demonstrated by Jennifer in this chapter. Could I emulate her example? Am I willing to adopt her approach for the next thirty days?
- Consider how practical and helpful the Daily Examen can be for my prayer life. Will I accept the challenge to put the Daily Examen on my calendar right now (see Appendix 2)? Am I willing to practice the Daily Examen faithfully every day for a month? Six months?

Author's Note:

With regard to the Daily Examen, place it as a daily occurrence on the calendar of the computer or hand-held device you use and set it up to remind you of each of the five brief periods of prayer and reflection required. I recommend 6:45 a.m., 10 a.m., 1:15 p.m., 5:30 p.m. and 9 p.m. Commit to following the Examen. It will be a tremendous addition to your prayer life.

CHAPTER 5

What's LOVE Got to Do With It?

> *Our personal struggles often become obstacles to helping our brothers and sisters in Christ.*

HOW OFTEN do we have an opportunity to be involved in the lives of our coworkers? Do we have the trust and rapport necessary to allow comfortable dialogues about serious personal issues? Just as we don't cease being Catholic when we get to work, our team members don't cease to be human beings deserving of our love when they get to work.

Paige Barry is an example of a loving leader, which seems like a rare thing in today's world. She is a senior vice president with a global, multibillion-dollar technology provider of information management and electronic commerce systems for the financial services industry. A lifelong Catholic, devoted wife, and mother of two children, Paige fully believes in the integration of her faith into every aspect of her life, especially work. One of the things that clearly separates her from many other business people I know is the selfless and loving attitude she brings to every conversation, decision, and action. It manifests itself in her patient listening to her team members, getting to know them personally, the coaching she provides to solve difficult problems, and the jobs ministry she runs at her parish, among other things. The Greeks called this type of selfless love *agape*, and it is the magic elixir that should drive our daily work activities.

Paige has countless opportunities to provide loving leadership to her large team on a daily basis, but she says her favorite example is an experience helping the daughter of a member of her team: "In 2010, God gave me an opportunity to live my faith out loud at work. An associate shared with me that her daughter was pregnant, and the pregnancy was not planned. Her daughter intended to have an abortion, which just broke the associate's heart. I told her that I would pray for her and her daughter, and I did. In less than forty-eight hours, the daughter changed her mind; and her son was born in October. I was blessed with the amazing experience of engaging Right to Life resources in Florida to provide the assistance the pregnant mother needed. I spoke to complete strangers who provided shelter, medical assistance, and transportation to someone who really needed the help."

Though we all aren't faced with this type of experience, it does have reflective value for us. Like Paige, we have the power of prayer, but not of a person's free will. Though Paige was physically helpless in this situation, her prayers to God were powerful enough that God's plan ultimately came through, and through that experience she saw an opportunity to help women like the daughter. Sometimes a prayer is all that is needed for a person to realize what her duties are to God and to life.

In addition to this powerful example of showing love in the

workplace, Paige has also had the opportunity of becoming the leader of the Little Flower Job Network, which provides job-search assistance and coaching to hundreds of job seekers each year. This valuable ministry enables Paige to help in a meaningful and loving way the numerous job seekers she meets or is referred to on a frequent basis.

It is by acting in a selfless and charitable way toward others and putting their needs before our own that people will truly begin to see Jesus in us. It is so easy to focus on our own desires and needs. Thus, our challenge is to make today about serving others. Let's reflect on the selfless examples of Paige Barry and others we know as inspiration for us to act the same way. Even little acts of selfless kindness will have a dramatic impact.

Chris Lowney, author of *Heroic Leadership: Best Practices From a 450-Year-Old Company*, wrote: "Love enables any company to welcome every sort of talent, irrespective of religion, race, social position, or credentials. Love is the joy of seeing team members succeed. Leaders motivated by love start from the premise that people will give their best when they work for those who provide genuine support and affection."[9]

In these difficult times, it can be very challenging to think of others and not just ourselves. Our personal struggles often become obstacles to helping our brothers and sisters in Christ. If these words resonate with you, I encourage you to break out of this inward focus and consider your Christian obligation to love and serve one another. It has been said that having the determination to help others will make our hearts bigger and bring us out of ourselves. There are no excuses for not helping others (for instance, lack of time, fear of becoming involved, or worrying about others). With that feeling of earnest determination, we are able to become helpful to others in prayer, such as Paige did (and does) for those in her life.

Like Paige, much of the earliest Christian communities showed love and charity toward one another. It is written that they lived the teachings of Christ in a way that serves as a model for how we can and should live our lives today. Our problems would not seem so great if we could count on the love and help of our brothers and sisters and they, in turn, could count on us.

In Saint Paul's Letter to the Galatians, he wrote: "Bear one another's burdens, and so you will fulfill the law of Christ" (Galatians 6:2). Sharing the burdens of those around us is vitally important, but so is encouraging them to remain strong in their walk of faith. Often adversity can weaken a person's relationship with Christ when these very obstacles should bring us closer to him. He is the great comforter to anyone who is struggling and offers love and a sense of peace to anyone who calls on him for help. Jesus said: "Come to me, all you who labor and are burdened, and I will give you rest. Take my yoke upon you and learn from me, for I am meek and humble of heart; and you will find rest for your selves. For my yoke is easy, and my burden light" (Matthew 11:28–30).

I would like to pose a challenge to all of us to think carefully about five powerful words that will serve as a catalyst for helping others the way our early Christian predecessors did: seeking, listening, loving, prayer, and charity.

We often don't know the people in our community or our workplace who need our help. Because of that, seeking them out will require us to observe more carefully and show a genuine, deeper interest in other people's lives. Let's transform "how are you doing?" from a superficial greeting into a sincere desire to understand what is going on in the lives of our coworkers, friends, family, and fellow parishioners. We need to slow down and be genuinely interested in others at the water cooler and the elevator as well as the narthex after Mass. Also, if we are sincere and transparent about our own challenges, we will likely see others feel more comfortable in opening up to us.

Listening is critical. When someone is willing to open up to you, don't interrupt with solutions right away. I struggle with this one. I have personally experienced some wonderful conversations with work colleagues in need of help who were eager to unburden themselves to someone who genuinely cared. Listening patiently and just being a friend can be a great source of comfort. It is important to note that others may open up to you more easily if you are willing to be transparent and share your own struggles as well. Listening is an active action. By listening, you will be a help to the person and a faithful coworker.

Our loving actions as Christians should always be motivated by a desire to encourage and help others and place their needs before our own. Love also precludes acting in a judgmental way. To understand love as it pertains to the workplace, reflect on the words of Jesus: "I give you a new commandment: love one another. As I have loved you, so you also should love one another. This is how all will know that you are my disciples, if you have love for one another" (John 13:34–35). In the early days of Christianity, Christians set themselves apart by how much they loved one another. Can the same be said of us today?

Praying for others is an absolute necessity. I encourage all of us to make sure we pray daily for those in need of help and that God will work through us to provide that help. If we say we will pray for someone, we need to honor that commitment. I often feel like such a novice at prayer, but I am certain that it is pleasing to God when we pray in earnest for others and their needs.

Charity is the best way to sow good all around us. Charity is one of the three theological virtues (along with faith and hope), and as the catechism (1827) says, "The practice of all the virtues is animated and inspired by charity, which 'binds everything together in perfect harmony'; it is the form of the virtues; it articulates and orders them among themselves; it is the source and the goal of their

Christian practice. Charity upholds and purifies our human ability to love, and raises it to the supernatural perfection of divine love."[10]

In order to fully understand these five words and how they fit into our lives and in our workplace, it is important to encompass them in and out of work. Doing so will help us live out our Christian faith in all facets of our lives so that we do not have to "check our faith at the door." Here is a challenge to you to practice these actions daily and to demonstrate through these an ongoing love for God and others:

1. **Help** job seekers meet people in your personal network who may be helpful in their search for a new career (see Appendix 3).

2. **Visit** one sick person at his home or in the hospital each month.

3. **Call** or send a card (or both) to those people for whom you are truly thankful and share with them how grateful you are to have them in your life.

4. **Organize** your work colleagues to adopt needy families, and make the lives of those families better with what you share at Christmas.

5. **Work** at a soup kitchen or visit a retirement home with your coworkers and family.

6. **Make** donations of used clothing, toys, books, or other useful items over the holidays. Our discarded items may be treasures to someone in need.

7. **Practice** "active listening" with your friends, fellow parishioners, and work colleagues with no agenda over a casual lunch or coffee meeting. Get beneath the surface and understand their personal challenges a little better.

8. **Pray** every day for those who are struggling.

9. **Invest** the time to teach our children about servant leadership

and selflessly helping others. One day they will do as adults what they learn in these formative years.

10. **Invite** someone who has fallen away from the Church to Mass or any of the special events in your parish community. Please remember to extend the invitation with love, not judgment.

My family, friends, work colleagues, and the needy of our community deserve and require all the selfless, charitable love I can offer. I like to think that I am always willing to help others, but I can do more. I have to let people see Christ's love at work in me, and I must learn to always see Christ in them. When you take these actions out into your own lives and your own communities, reflect on the words of the Apostle John, "Beloved, let us love one another, because love is of God; everyone who loves is begotten by God and knows God" (1 John 4:7). On that, you must also be willing to act in a loving way toward those whose views you oppose. It is important to speak up, but in a respectful and compassionate way, even if you are not being given the same courtesy.

When you consider the thoughts of this chapter, think about what they mean to you, but also what your thoughts and actions mean to those around you. As many of us work through our own personal struggles, it is sometimes difficult to keep the focus on Christ and helping others. Don't be put off by real or imagined rigid company guidelines that become an excuse for us to not lovingly engage with people at work. Remember that in the end, the selfless help we provide to others becomes a grace-filled gift...to us.

REFLECTION AND DISCUSSION

- Before reading this chapter, had I ever considered the concept of "love" in the workplace?
- Does Paige's example resonate with me? What opportunities have I had in the past to demonstrate *agape* love? Did I make the most of those opportunities?
- Reflect on the ten actions listed in this chapter. Is this list achievable? What can I commit to doing? What would I add to this list? I will prayerfully consider sharing a list of my commitments to serve others with friends and ask them to hold me accountable... and to join me in my efforts.

CHAPTER 6

Being Good Stewards

"As each one has received a gift, use it to serve one another as good stewards of God's varied grace" (1 Peter 4:10).

Go to Christ in prayer each day and ask for his will to be revealed and for direction on how to best serve him.

THE TRADITIONAL DEFINITION of stewardship you have likely heard is to give your time, talent, and treasure to help others. Good stewards take excellent care of whatever gifts or talents they have been entrusted with and use them in the service of others. The U.S. Catholic Bishops said it best in *Stewardship: A Disciple's Response*: "(A Christian steward is) one who receives God's gifts gratefully, cherishes and tends them in a responsible and accountable manner, shares them in justice and love with others, and returns them with increase to the Lord."[11]

When we take this general understanding of stewardship and apply it to the workplace, we begin to see it on a more personal and interactive level. As we go through this chapter, continue to think about the previous chapter and how love played a role in your faith/work integration. By the end of this chapter, I hope that you will have a better understanding of love and stewardship in the workplace and how both are necessary to a fuller faith life.

When we think of workplace stewardship, we think of others both in and outside of our work environments. For example, Terry Trout is the vice president of customer experience for a national company that delivers integrated packages of communications and IT services to thousands of small businesses throughout the U.S. She is a legend in her community, with a long track record of nonprofit board service for a variety of great causes, a passion for mentoring others, and a strong desire to pay it forward. Terry is also a lifelong Catholic and is very active in her parish. She sums up her philosophy on stewardship with this insight: "I am best served when I am serving others. The world is a great mirror. It reflects back to me what I give. When I am optimistic, generous and helpful, my world will prove to be successful, supportive, and overflowing. When I am short, spiteful, or driven (and I can be all three), I find my world reacts with those same ugly tendencies. My world is what I am."

Terry clearly understands that being a good steward is more than simply writing a check or donating online. Her perspective is all-encompassing, and she gives of her time, talent, and treasure freely, but also thoughtfully. She is very self-aware about her skills, gifts, and limits as she chooses where she can make a difference in the lives of others.

"When people ask me how I can find time to give back, I encourage them to recognize that each of us has something to offer, whatever time, whatever talent to the degree the season of our life allows. When my girls were little, it was about engaging at church, with soccer, and at their school. At one point, all I could manage was serving as a eucharistic minister. Now as an empty-nester, I can give more freely. As an executive, I can bring to bear resources, services, and networking. Every organization I have ever helped has been eager and grateful for anything I could offer, and I have come to believe that it is incumbent on us to each find that opportunity to raise our hand. I know that answering that calling has expanded my world, my network, and my energy level. I would never have imagined the friends, experiences, and professional development that I have been gifted through volunteering and serving others."

Terry has integrated "giving back" into her daily routine and leadership style. Her successful efforts are our call to action to use our gifts for others. "As each one has received a gift, use it to serve one another as good stewards of God's varied grace" (1 Peter 4:10). While Terry displays strong stewardship, she also reflects back through her actions a love for what she does and what she does for others. In her acts of stewardship, she is able to reach out through her faith to others and continue to be a wonderful example of what stewards we should be in and out of work.

How do we become Catholic stewards of our time, talent, and treasure in the workplace? First, let's address the obstacles to our workplace stewardship before I offer some proactive ideas and solutions. I have discussed this topic with Catholic professionals over the years, and five basic obstacles consistently emerge:

- "I donate at my parish and am active there. Why do I need to do it at work?"
- "I am too busy."
- "I already spend time at the company's quarterly service project."
- "I don't really understand what I can do to practice Catholic stewardship. I am not sure where to begin."

- "If I am being honest, I worry that people will ask more of me than I am able to give."

Do these obstacles/excuses resonate with you? Perhaps you are following Terry's stellar example, or you may have additional obstacles to add to the list. If you aren't already following Terry's example, let's consider shifting our mindsets and expanding our thinking to the true nature of stewardship by looking at these practical actions that will help us improve in this important area.

Stewardship does not need to be an either/or exercise. True stewardship, especially Catholic stewardship, needs to be integrated into our lives; this includes our work lives. Just as we can't leave our faith at the door when we arrive at work, we can't leave our obligations to help others outside either. The "pay it forward" mantra so popular today is completely applicable to the concept of stewardship. What we do outside of work is often reflected in who we become at work. Simply put, we need to offer to help others before seeking anything in return. In fact, try to let go of having any expectation of return. Achieving this true selflessness has its rewards, far greater than any acknowledgment here on earth. God will always bless selfless acts done in his name.

When you think about stewardship in and out of the workplace, consider the perspective I learned from Charlie Douglas, a Catholic and a senior executive with a national financial services company: "Corporate stewardship begins with the mindset that our duties to shareholders, customers, and the community are best discharged when we see ourselves as God's trustee. Much like the laborers in the Lord's vineyards, we, too, are called to a high standard of management in the marketplace. As faithful stewards, it takes more than just simply seeking to maximize profits through self-interest. It takes an understanding that we have a responsibility beyond the immediate marketplace, and beyond providing for only our family's wants and needs. It is inspiring to know that when we go to work in association with others we can positively influence and impact the unspoken needs of many both here and abroad."

Charlie's point is clear: We have a responsibility to be good stewards in the communities where we operate our businesses. Donating to earn a tax break is not enough. We are accountable for using our influence, expertise, and time to leave a lasting legacy of good works.

Unfortunately, we often get hung up on the treasure part of stewardship and write our checks or donate online to seemingly fulfill our stewardship duties. Don't get me wrong: Money is vitally important to fund great causes. But we may be ignoring the other important aspects of stewardship, especially in the workplace. Are we listening to a troubled coworker who shares his or her problems? Are we helping our friends in career transition find new employment? Are we organizing volunteer efforts in our companies to help good causes? Do we spend time mentoring and coaching younger employees? Are we volunteering for nonprofit boards where our particular expertise can be an asset? Are we inspiring those around us to do the same? The point is, we have ample opportunities to practice Catholic stewardship if we only look around us, focus on being selfless and show genuine love for our neighbors or coworkers. These efforts don't always affect our checkbooks and credit cards, and they should all start with a simple human interaction fueled by a desire to serve others.

We have read about Terry Trout's good stewardship example, and Charlie Douglas provided valuable perspective. We have, I hope, changed our mindsets. Now, let's explore practical ideas for integrating Catholic stewardship into our work lives. I propose four steps for achieving this goal that can be adopted immediately:

1. Pray for discernment.

Go to Christ in prayer each day and ask for his will to be revealed and for direction on how to best serve him. Ask for the awareness to know where the needs are and how you can help. Here is more insight from Charlie Douglas: "Prayer today is so often about informing God of our wishes and our will. The truth is, however, that prayer is about conforming our will to God's. Jesus made this clear in the Garden of Gethsemane when he earnestly prayed that above all his Father's will be done. And part of our Father's will is to sacrificially carry our crosses in service to the homeless, the poor, the despondent, and the unloved. To be the hands and feet of Christ to the Lazaruses all around us is a beautiful prayer."

2. Know your gifts and talents.

Make an inventory of what you can offer others. If you don't know, ask for candid and honest feedback from people who know you well. Understanding your talents will enable you to better apply yourself in the service of others. Consider the impact of your organizational skills on a dysfunctional nonprofit or how your passion for carpentry can help build a house for Habitat for Humanity. Maybe your influence can bring disparate groups together to achieve noble goals in the community. Or your great capacity for kindness may make a significant difference in the lives of the unemployed in your circle. We all have gifts, and they can all find value in serving those in need.

3. Be present...and act today.

Watch, listen, and act. Look daily for opportunities to help family, friends, coworkers, and strangers. Someone is struggling at this very moment with any number of personal challenges. Because we spend the majority of our adult lives at work, our best opportunity to help others directly may be through our work colleagues. But we often feel that we don't have time to get involved or that we have enough problems to handle. Let's ask the Holy Spirit to help us discern who needs our help today and to use our time wisely, for the greatest good. Don't wait until tomorrow.

4. Serve quietly and be humble.

Serving others is not always about padding our résumés with nonprofit board roles or leading fund-raising campaigns. Our most effective moments of stewardship may very well come in the hushed conversation with a troubled coworker, the introduction we make for someone in career transition to our network, or the "good morning" we say to the person on the elevator who may be having a bad day. As Christ said, "(But) take care not to perform righteous deeds in order that people may see them; otherwise, you will have no recompense from your heavenly Father. When you give alms, do not blow a trumpet before you, as the hypocrites do in the synagogues and in the streets to win the praise of others. Amen, I say to you, they have received their reward. But when you give alms, do not let your left hand know what your right is doing, so that your almsgiving may be secret. And your Father who sees in secret will repay you" (Matthew 6:1–4). It is your goal to go out each day and show your stewardship not expecting anything in return. Nor should anything be done in exchange for praise.

Catholic stewardship, when approached with a spirit of sincerity and joy, can be wonderfully contagious! I know many people such as Terry Trout and Charlie Douglas who inspire those around them in the workplace to take the first steps toward serving others merely through their excellent example.

I believe a majority of us want to help others and that most of us are well-intended. Try to reflect at different points each day on your actions toward others and examine any missed opportunities to help someone who is struggling so you can attend to them later. Expanded thinking and active engagement are required. Let's evolve our good intentions to a higher standard and begin to recognize those in need more clearly and frequently. Let's make our first words: "Please let me help you."

REFLECTION AND DISCUSSION

- Reflect on how I currently use my time, talent, and treasure to serve God and others. Could I do more?
- Terry has a clear idea of where she can add the most value. Have I reflected on this for myself? Where can I make a significant difference in my Catholic stewardship?
- Often our daily stewardship can be reflected in our actions toward those around us. This can range from a friendly greeting in the elevator to connecting a job seeker to someone in our network. Have I missed opportunities to "pay it forward" with people I encounter each day? I will commit to the practical step of placing a reminder on my calendar to serve others every day and watch the ripple effect of my actions positively affect the people around me.
- How can I be a better steward in my company? How can I influence my coworkers and company leaders to get involved in helping worthy causes?

CHAPTER 7

Leading by Example

> *Authenticity is the*
> *foundation of example.*

DAVID MCCULLOUGH is a senior leader of a company that provides software and services to consumer-lending organizations throughout North America and the United Kingdom. He is a devoted husband and the proud father of three children. A convert to Catholicism several years ago, David has fully embraced his faith in every area of his life, especially the workplace. As I was considering candidates for this chapter of the book, David was the first person who came to mind. I recently had an opportunity to interview him and discuss his thoughts on faith at work and setting a good example for others to follow.

Q. David, how does your Catholic faith influence you at work?

A. My Catholic faith is intertwined with all aspects of my life, including my hours at the office. Whether it is at a time when a difficult decision needs to be made, or a moment when a coworker needs someone to talk to, I know that my faith guides me. Each day I try to be a good steward of the gifts that God has given me. I work knowing that nothing belongs to me, not the job itself, not the money associated with it, not even the success that I have seen over the years. It is all his. My prayer each day when I arise is that I be the man that Christ Jesus wants me to be that day and that I use the talents that he has given me to shine his light throughout my world.

Q. What can you share about how you set a good example for others because of your Catholic faith?

A. I am a pretty transparent guy. What you see is what you get with me. Most, if not all, of my coworkers know that I am Catholic. They know because I talk about it. I am actively involved in the ministries of my parish, and I share the news regarding the good works that are taking place in the Archdiocese. They know that I am Christ-centered and that truth and justice are paramount to me. Sure, there are outward signs that give example to my being a Catholic. Maybe it is the sign of the cross and a prayer before a meal, or a water-cooler discussion regarding the work the night before at the Catholic homeless shelter; but to me it is the inward signs that are equally important. The example I set in my attitude, my demeanor, and my approach to difficult situations hopefully sets a positive example for others. I have Christ in my heart, and that truly makes a difference, not only for me, but for all those who Christ allows me to touch.

Q. Why is it important for you to be authentic about your Catholic faith?

A. I grew up in the South, but I did not grow up Catholic. I was baptized Southern Methodist and then spent most of my teenage years attending the Presbyterian Church. Some of my closest friends growing up were Catholic, and I always remember them being devout and staunch in their beliefs, especially regarding the Eucharist. I married a Catholic in 1996 and joined the Church in 2003. Coming out of the RCIA program into full communion with the Church, I realized how important it was that I maintained my newfound Catholic identity and that I be authentic about it. I truly believe that a "lukewarm" Christian is a stone's throw from an agnostic, and I had no intention of going down that path. I jumped right into the ministries within my parish, and I have never looked back. While I am not what you might call a radical evangelist, I have been told that I set a positive example for other Catholics. What a beautiful compliment. Authenticity is the foundation of that example. If you are not authentic in all that you do, especially in your faith, then you are merely a "resounding gong or a clashing cymbal" (1 Corinthians 13:1).

Q. How are others in your business life/circle positively affected by your Catholicism?

A. I have had the blessing of being told on more than one occasion that my Catholicism has been a comfort to those I work with. I remember vividly a coworker telling me that the example Christ allowed me to be in her life inspired her return to the sacrament of reconciliation more than a decade after leaving the Church. I recently had a former coworker call me and tell me that he had been praying about their faith and contacted me because he knew that I was a firm believer in the Catholic Church and the power of the

Eucharist. This young man went on to say that he and his wife were interested in finding out more about the Church, and he thought that he was being called to become a Catholic. I was truly honored to be able to share a meal with them and discuss what "being Catholic" is all about. What a blessing to be able to share my faith with others.

Q. *What do you do or try to do daily in the form of prayer, Mass attendance, etc., that you integrate into your workday?*

A. The foundation for my personal practice of integration is the people I choose to surround myself with at work and in my circle of friends. It has been said that you can look at those you associate with and can almost guarantee that you will be like them in less than five years. With that thought in mind, I try to surround myself with the most spiritual, giving, brightest stars in the Catholic community. When I look around, I see priests, deacons, and laypeople who really "get it." If I can merely stand in their shadow, then there is a chance that I can get one step closer to being the strongest Catholic possible. I attend Mass during the workday as often as possible. It is amazing how everything comes back into perspective after you attend Mass on a workday. Nothing gets you more centered than the presence of the Eucharist. In addition, daily prayer puts me in the presence of Christ each day. The Jesuit Daily Examen is an excellent way to get a prayer routine introduced into your life (see Appendix 2). And remember, prayer isn't just about mealtime and bedtime; prayer should be woven into every aspect of our lives. Just the other day my twelve-year-old son came to me and said, "Dad, can we pray about my game today? I have a bad feeling and I am nervous." So, I had the opportunity to hug my child and pray with him that Christ would use the talents that he gave him to the best of his ability. We praised and thanked him and asked that whatever the outcome of the game, he use this day for his greater glory. If you know of a better experience a parent can have with (his) child than going to our Lord and Savior in prayer together, I want to know what it is!

David provides us with a wonderful perspective on how to live faithfully at work and to use that faith in every facet of life. Many of us want to follow David's excellent example but don't know how. What is holding us back? In speaking with friends and professional acquaintances about openly sharing our Catholic faith, I have always been a little surprised at how many of them express strong reluctance to being open about their beliefs. The reasons given include, "We are not allowed to do that at work," "I don't want to offend anyone," and "I don't like to discuss that outside of my parish." A central theme runs through their responses, and it has been the impetus for a lot of my reflection and prayer that has gone into this chapter:

- Do we ever stop to consider how many times a day our thinking and actions regarding our Catholic faith are influenced by a misguided concern for what others think of us?
- Do we miss opportunities to stand up for Christ or share our faith? Is it the conversation we avoid with a troubled coworker? Is it our refusal to publicly make the sign of the cross and say a blessing over our meals? Is it failing to stand up to someone who is attacking the Church? How about the person who is quietly curious about the Catholic faith and is only waiting for an invitation to attend Mass with us? Too often a misplaced concern for the opinions of those around us keeps us from embracing our responsibilities. However, it is crystal clear that Jesus expects us to openly share our faith and acknowledge him before others: "Everyone who acknowledges me before others I will acknowledge before my heavenly Father. But whoever denies me before others,

I will deny before my heavenly Father" (Matthew 10:32–33). From Jesus, we learn that being a faithful Catholic in the workplace is not something to be ashamed of or to hide. In fact, it makes us who we are in the workplace and creates the person we are.

Christ is our greatest example of how to not be concerned about the respect of others. He always taught the truth, regardless of the audience or his surroundings. His enemies recognized this aspect of Christ's teaching in Matthew 22:16, "Teacher, we know that you are a truthful man and that you teach the way of God in accordance with the truth. And you are not concerned with anyone's opinion, for you do not regard a person's status."

Francis Fernandez, author of *In Conversation With God*, makes this observation about courageously sharing the truth: "Christ asks his disciples to imitate him in this practice. Christians should foster and defend their well-earned professional, moral, and social prestige, since it belongs to the essence of human dignity. This prestige is also an important component of our personal apostolate. Yet we should not forget that our conduct will meet with opposition from those who openly oppose Christian morality and those who practice a watered-down version of the faith. It is possible that the Lord will ask of us the sacrifice of our good name, and even of life itself. With the help of his grace we will struggle to do his will. Everything we have belongs to the Lord."[12]

He goes on to say that in a difficult situation, we should not give in to the temptation of simply taking the easy way out, for it may lead us away from God. Instead, he calls us to always make the decision that strengthens our faith and holds onto our deepest convictions. How we act in difficult situations, and every day for that matter, reflects the type of Christian we are. I would suggest that not taking a stand for Christ and not openly sharing our true beliefs may be one of the biggest obstacles for many of us in growing in our faith…and possibly for those around us who are watching our example.

But it's not an uncommon trait to see in people. After all, who wants to risk any work relationships because of faith? Chances are you have struggled with worrying about what others think of you. It is a natural human tendency that affects me and everyone I know. We all want to be liked, respected, and included. But here's the catch: We can't separate our spiritual selves from our physical being. The faith we profess is part of who we are and can't be hidden away. If you remember back to the introduction, I pointed out a document from the Second Vatican Council that points out a dichotomy between the faith we profess and what we actually practice. It emphasized the tendency to ignore the value of our faith in order to appease ourselves.

The more you are able to profess your faith, the easier it will be to carry out the actions of that faith. So here are five thoughts on how to overcome our fear of what others may think of us and go about setting a good example:

1. Show me that in the policy manual.

I have heard many times that expressing faith in the workplace is "against company policy." Have you actually seen a written policy addressing making the sign of the cross and praying at meals, praying quietly at your desk, going to Mass at lunch, or wearing ashes on your forehead on Ash Wednesday? Let me challenge all of us to consider the possibility that much of our fear may be based on a false perception of possible persecution and not reality. Therefore, use your right to live your life as faithfully as you possibly can. In doing so, you will not only find work more enjoyable, but you will inspire others to do the same.

2. Witness through personal example.

Think about your own faith journey, how you got to where you are, how you live it day to day with something new to look forward to when you head into work. Think about the example that you could set for others and the strong faith you can radiate onto others. Letting others see Jesus Christ at work in us is a powerful form of witness that will attract others who want what we have in our lives. We are always being observed by someone. Will our actions inspire them or disappoint them? "You are the salt of the earth....You are the light of the world. A city set on a mountain cannot be hidden. Just so, your light must shine before others, that they may see your good deeds and glorify your heavenly Father" (Matthew 5:13–14, 16). Think about your actions and how they can inspire others to live as faithfully as you do. Be careful, however, as you do not want your actions to be of a selfish nature. Love as Jesus teaches, and others will follow.

3. Start the conversation with a little sharing of our own.

Transparency invites transparency. We can't expect someone to open up to us unless we are willing to do the same. Our faith journey is a blessing, meant to be shared. The witness we give may have a profound influence on someone. As we read in 1 Peter 3:15–16: "Always be ready to give an explanation to anyone who asks you for a reason for your hope, but do it with gentleness and reverence, keeping your conscience clear, so that, when you are maligned, those who defame your good conduct in Christ may themselves be put to shame." While you are eager to share your faith with others, we are warned here to do so with care and with a gentle love.

4. Reality check: Pursuing heaven versus being popular.

Heaven is our ultimate destination and not this place called earth. Will our critics help us get to heaven? Will they stand up for us during tough times? No, they will pull us into a secular way of life that has little room for God and where materialism and popularity are the fashionable idols of the day. Francis Fernandez wrote that overcoming human respect is part of the virtue of fortitude. He describes the challenges a Christian may endure as false, often in the sense that our relationships at work become superficial, and we lose out on financial opportunities, and so on. As discussed earlier, in uncomfortable and difficult situations it can be too tempting to take the easy way out and to give in. In doing that, we often feel that we are avoiding rejection and ridicule. Yet, Fernandez goes on to say that when we do that, we close the door for opportunities to grow in the future. We end up hiding our real identity and forsake our commitment to live as disciples of Christ. Doing what is right is not always easy, but in the long run it is the most beneficial.

5. Be consistent and lead an integrated Catholic life.

Do we take our faith with us to work, meals with friends, the kids' soccer games, and neighborhood swim meets? Or, do we only practice our Catholic faith at Mass on Sunday? It is easy to conform to secular expectations but difficult to publicly lead a fully integrated life. I have always found inspiration on this topic from the wisdom of John Paul II's apostolic exhortation, *Christifideles Laici*: "The fundamental objective of the formation of the lay faithful is an ever-clearer discovery of one's vocation and the ever-greater willingness to live it so as to fulfill one's mission....The lay faithful, in fact, are called by God so that they, led by the spirit of the Gospel, might contribute to the sanctification of the world, as from within like leaven, by fulfilling their own particular duties. Thus, especially in this way of life, resplendent in faith, hope, and charity they manifest Christ to others."[13]

We can't do this alone, and we must pray for the guidance of the Holy Spirit. In my own experience, this is a daily work-in-progress, and it is never easy. But we should all recognize that there are people looking at us to see our example. They want to learn from and be inspired by our courage, if we are willing to take a stand for Christ. Think about how fortunate we are to live in a country that believes in religious freedom (although our religious liberties are under attack), where all we risk is a little disapproval or alienation from others. When we take our faith to work, we are standing up to that fear and solidifying the core values that we as Christians believe in. In order to maintain that strength, it is important to live faithfully each and every day, which means taking that faith to work. It will be difficult at times and will require sacrifice, but to live with the love of God every minute of every day is far more rewarding than a little disapproval.

I know this is difficult, but the sacrifice is required. The sacrifice is simply to love Christ more than we love the opinions of those around us. Let's pray for one another and continue to ask Jesus for courage, strength, and the discernment to know and follow his will and not be concerned about the opinions of others. What kind of personal example will we set tomorrow?

REFLECTION AND DISCUSSION

- Have I ever considered that the example I set in the workplace could be one of the best ways to share my Catholic faith? A positive example will attract others and potentially build the foundation for engagement that will have a positive influence in people's lives and their faith journeys. Reflect on the example I have been setting for others and seek to make improvements.
- Is it difficult to be authentic in the workplace? Can someone ever set a good example without being authentic, especially with regard to his faith? Why? Why not?
- How often do I worry about what others think of me? How does this affect my actions about being open about my Catholic faith?
- It has been said that leaders often walk a lonely road. Setting a good example as a Catholic in the workplace will sometimes require sacrifice and courage. Am I prepared to risk my popularity with coworkers and friends to stand by my convictions? Reflect on my willingness to make this sacrifice. What is my commitment going forward?

CHAPTER 8

Better Decision-Making

> *So many times, including very painful*
> *moments or situations in business, there*
> *is a lot that appears to not be going right.*

DAVID MURPHY is a Catholic husband and father with a passion for serving others. He is the chairman of Better World Books, a company that collects and sells books online to fund literacy initiatives worldwide. With more than eight million new and used titles in stock, it is a self-sustaining, triple-bottom-line company that creates social, economic, and environmental value for all of its stakeholders. What makes David an outstanding candidate to be featured in this chapter, in addition to the good work he does with Better World Books, are his humility and his initial reluctance to be included in the book because he felt he was unworthy.

I met with David recently in between his frequent trips around the country where he meets with client partners and speaks to top business schools about his company's mission. This interview with

David captures perfectly the concept of "better decision-making" through the eyes of a humble Catholic leader.

Q. David, how does your Catholic faith influence your decision-making at work? Does it help you make better decisions?

A. Every morning I try and attend Mass, as well as read the Scripture readings for that day and some meditation/reflection on the readings. Being able to participate in the Mass, receive the miracle of the Eucharist, and take some quiet time to pray, reflect, and give my day to God puts me in the right mindset to let God take control and let me simply be his humble, faithful, and obedient servant; to implore him to lead and guide me this day for his greater glory; that his will be done, not mine. I also try and make sure that I am thanking God each morning for the tremendous blessings in my life, and being specific with him about what I am thankful for. The list can be a mile long....It hits the basics that we so often take for granted: "Thank you for my wife and children and grandchild, for their health and safety, that we were all able to sleep last night in safety with a roof over our heads, that we have clean water and food, that none of us is hungry, that we have the gift of education and work, that we live in a country and in a community that is safe and free (and for all of the men and women who lay their lives on the line each and every day for that to happen...and their families)"; etc. I always think of one Scripture passage that drives this home for me: Luke's account of the ten lepers and the one (in ten) who returns to actually thank the Lord for being healed. I find that heading in to work my mind is more calm, more focused on doing God's will in all that I do and say, with all whom I will meet and speak with, with all of the decisions I will make.

I am not sure if all of my decisions are better because of this. Certainly I have made my fair share of mistakes and "wrong calls."

But I do believe that our time, our way, our definition of successful decision-making (which is most often determined in the immediate) is not God's way; it is not his definition of success. So what I may think is an absolutely great decision may turn out that way in the short term. Or over time it may not look so good. And vice versa: What I thought was a good decision may turn out not to be so great in the very near term, but over time it appears to be more wise. In either situation, the key for me is to always implore God's assistance, his divine intervention before, during, and after a key decision, and trust it to him.

So many times, including very painful moments or situations in business, there is a lot that appears to not be going right. Have I been able to look back with the benefit of hindsight…in some cases years of hindsight…and seen the hand of God at work in a way that was ultimately the very best thing for me and for the business?

I do know that when I have totally trusted in God, when I have truly been at peace with him and his work, that I have hired better people, I have communicated with employees better, I have been more calm, more truly authentic and "servant" in my leadership. I have connected better with key strategic partners and actually closed deals that initially were perceived as "long shots," all from just trying, as best as I am able, to turn it over to God, to let him drive, to let him provide all of the direction, clarity, and storytelling that needs to be told. When we really truly give it to God, amazing things can happen.

Q. How are others in your business life/circle positively affected by your Catholicism?

A. First of all, not enough. This gets back to my comments to you about feeling so unworthy in many cases to even be speaking on this subject. I do think when I am totally giving everything to God to let his will be done through me, that I am more calm, much more anxiety-free, much less likely to fly off the handle and end up making ill-advised, short-term decisions that, in the end, do not deliver the results I was hoping for. I have, throughout my career, heard things like, "You are so calm in the middle of a very trying, turbulent situation. How do you do that?" Or, "Wow. There are so many great things going on with your company, and yet you seem content to not try and grab the headlines. You let others lead. You let others get the credit." And I know this is directly related to my faith and what Scripture teaches us about humility (and) servant leadership (Jesus washing the feet of the apostles on Holy Thursday). Probably one of my favorite Scripture passages here is the story of Peter walking on water to see our Lord. He is fine for a while, but the minute he doubts, the minute he wavers, he starts to sink. And the Lord saves him. So at work, with each and every situation I face, good or bad, simple or complex, with colleagues or alone, do they see a confident "Peter" walking toward our Lord? Or do they see someone sinking, someone not surrendering to God's will but trying to figure everything out on his own? Do my employees, my customers, suppliers, board, and each and every stakeholder group whom I am there to serve, do they see a leader who is bent over washing their feet and who is truly serving them? Someone who is truly authentic?

I don't preach my Catholicism. I don't actively talk about it and push it. Here is where I actually think I could do more of this, that at times I am too quiet about it. So again, I struggle with my own imperfection. But I do want all who come in contact with me to see our Lord, to hear him, to feel him through all I do and say and am. I pray for this every morning. I am mindful of it throughout the day. I pause often and ask for his strength, his guidance and direction to reflect his love and compassion and strength in all that I do and say and am. Just being actively mindful of it and striving to attain that in the workplace is a positive and something I am trying to do more and more of each day.

Q. How do you integrate prayer, Mass attendance, etc., into your workday?

A. One thing I have been trying to do more of is to stop several times a day and simply take a minute or two to pray, to talk with God about something that is right in front of me, something that is troubling me, something that is problematic. Also, to thank him right on the spot for something that just happened that is good, that is an answer to a prayer. I am really trying to be so much more mindful of a commitment to trust our Lord (appropriate on Divine Mercy Sunday, "Jesus, I trust in you!"). I find myself more and more in a constant state of prayer, meditation, and dialogue with our Lord where I am trying to trust him, trying to understand what he wants me to do or say. And this is especially true in business with the myriad of complexities and challenges that spring up every day.

The interview continues, and what we can take from it will be endless. In a nutshell, David Murphy captures on so many levels the keys to better decision-making through the eyes of our Catholic faith. David thinks and acts with the heart of a humble servant leader, looking to God for strength in difficult times and being willing to admit and reflect on his mistakes so he does not repeat them. This makes very clearly the case for integrating faith and work. Would

David, or any of us for that matter, be able to make appropriate decisions if our Catholic faith was left at the door of our workplaces?

After speaking with David, I became more inquisitive about how to prioritize decisions into everyday life and what effects those decisions have on our lives and of others around us. After all, every decision has consequences, and those consequences typically involve people. But to gain more understanding, I sought the wisdom of another good friend, Charlie Douglas, whom I quote frequently in this book. I gleaned some excellent insight into this aspect during a recent conversation with him. Charlie is a Catholic husband, father, author, speaker, and a senior vice president for a leading financial services company. With absolute candor, he shared: "For me, work-place decisions are typically compromised by the daily stress and pressure to perform. Still, my best decisions occur when I am able to see past my own business interest and earnestly consider the interests of shareholders, customers, and coworkers alike. Many decisions I and others make impact others directly and indirectly. So I try as often as I can to say, if I decide "X" how might I feel about that if were in another person's shoes? If it seems like the right thing for me, where my own boat is likely to rise, will my decision help others and their boats to rise, too? In the end, it is not about trying to please all in making decisions, many of which are not clean and easy to make. It is about recognizing that we are called to advance the common good, not just our own good."

Charlie's point is that we must consider the broader view of our decisions and how they will impact others. Charlie looks to the good example of Blessed Teresa of Calcutta because of her efforts regarding solidarity and serving the poorest of the poor. He also prays the Devotion to the Divine Mercy Chaplet daily and studies the Church doctrines on social justice and *Centesimus Annus* because economic decisions are moral decisions, and he says we need to be mindful that our choices need to promote life, human dignity, and advance the common good. But in today's world, all of that becomes more of a challenge each day.

I do not consider myself a pessimist, but if we were to reflect at length on many of the problems affecting business today, we would likely feel discouraged and frustrated. At the heart of much of what I see as wrong is the compromised decision-making by business leaders, many of whom would ironically be likely to profess to having some degree of faith in their lives. Business can't survive without profit. We all understand this fundamental principle. But the pursuit of profit at the expense of people, ethics, and basic morality is a wrong that can be positively addressed if we make decisions through the lens of our Catholic faith.

As you reflect on this chapter and the way you currently make decisions, consider your answers to these questions:

How do I come across to others?
How am I perceived by my coworkers and clients?

Self-awareness is critical, and if you don't know, ask those around you for candid feedback. It is important to be authentic and natural even as we seek to improve. Avoid becoming someone you are not, but instead remain true to your values and your faith.

Am I able to detach myself from personal benefit
in my decisions?

Objectivity is important, but it is difficult when we are thinking about our own financial gain. We must live the virtue of integrity at all times, especially if we are decision-makers.

*Do I let fear of judgment by others get in the way
of making the right decisions?*

This is a common problem, but we should only be answerable to Christ. His opinion outweighs all others. Making the right decisions can, paradoxically, cost you everything if you are in the wrong environment. But, we will be answerable in heaven one day for our actions on this earth, and we must be diligent in doing the right and noble thing at all times.

Do I truly see Christ in others?

We will make better decisions if we consider the impact on people and see our Lord in each of them. Acting with *agape* love toward others is the key.

*Am I praying for guidance and wisdom
in my decision-making?*

The key is to not ask God to validate our decisions but to seek the guidance of the Holy Spirit in making good decisions. God should always be our most trusted counselor and advisor on important decisions.

There has been much to consider in this chapter in how we are currently making decisions. The above questions are a good way to check ourselves and take stock. We must always remember that we are made for heaven, and our actions in the workplace have enormous impact on where our journey will end.

REFLECTION AND DISCUSSION

- Have I ever viewed my Catholic faith as a filter through which I should make business decisions? Reflect on this idea and consider how I can integrate faith into how I think, act, and perform at work.
- One of the keys to David Murphy's success as a leader is his humility. Do others see me as humble? Why or why not? What can I do to sincerely show more humility?
- Do I ever consider the moral implications of my decisions in the workplace? Reflect on the points Charlie Douglas made in this chapter on how our decisions affect others. What positive changes can I make immediately?

CHAPTER 9

The Unconnected Catholic

> *Catholic business people who neglect their networks are missing out on a wonderful opportunity.*

BASED ON MY EXPERIENCE, Catholic business people could do a much better job of connecting and networking with one another. They are not unlike business people in general, who typically connect with others much less frequently as they grow in their careers. The Catholic businessperson, however, is missing much more than access to people during a possible career transition or to benefit their business. They are missing out on a supportive community. In this chapter, I will explore why this might be the case and what the Catholic businessperson can do to alleviate this.

Much of what you have read in this book has intended to challenge you to incorporate new ideas and different thinking into how you integrate faith at work. With regard to tapping into a supportive community, this may be even more difficult for those who would simply like to connect with a peer group for advice and counsel. Some may be in career transition and want to network with people they trust. Shared faith is a great foundation for building trust. Others may enjoy the fellowship of other Catholics. Whatever your reason, there is much to be gained from associating with your fellow Catholics from the business community outside of Mass. In this chapter we will uncover obstacles to Catholic connecting, the required investment, and some practical examples of opportunities to make these connections a reality.

THE OBSTACLES

Why is networking and connecting with fellow Catholics such a challenge? What gets in the way? There are five fundamental obstacles that surface on a consistent basis:

1. "I don't have enough time to network."

This is an obstacle that appears time and again, but it is the easiest to overcome, as you will see in the investment section of this chapter. This is simply a scheduling and commitment issue. Most people I have met in my professional life think this way but later regret their lack of attention to networking at some point in their lives. You will be more likely to "have time" if you schedule it. Take a client to lunch, invite coworkers out after work, or just send correspondence to somebody daily.

2. "I don't know how to identify other Catholics in the business community."

The Internet is a great source for finding Catholic business people in your area. Simply type in "Catholic business networking sites," or "business networking sites," in the search area to see what sites are available and most popular. There are many other ways to connect, which we cover later in this chapter.

3. "I am not sure I see the value in connecting with other Catholics outside of Mass. What's the point?"

Too often we live in a vacuum as Catholics and don't get enough opportunities to discuss our faith, our lives, or our challenges. Ask yourself whether you have all the prayers, encouragement, knowledge, support, and contacts you could ever use in your lifetime. Now do you see the value?

4. "I'm on social network and business network sites, so I am networking."

These helpful social media tools serve a useful purpose and can enhance networking. But they should not replace the face-to-face human interaction required in effective network building. Think of these electronic networks as a starting point to building stronger and long-lasting relationships.

5. "I'm not very good at making new connections, and adding my Catholic faith to it makes it even more intimidating."

This is a troublesome and common admission for many. Remember that networking can and should be tailored to your style and personality. The secret is to find the method that maximizes your strengths. Adding our Catholic faith to the equation should make it easier, not more difficult. You and the person you are networking with share something powerful and beautiful: the Catholic Church. What a great way to begin a conversation.

I find the best way to shift a pattern of thinking is to ask challenging questions. For example: Could I benefit from the example of others in the Catholic business community? Am I getting the faith development I need? Is my job secure? If not, do I have a network of people who can help me? Could I benefit from sharing knowledge and networks with others? Can I do more in the parish and larger community by working with fellow Catholics in my diocese? If you answered "yes" to any of these questions, this chapter was written for you.

THE INVESTMENT

OK, you understand the importance of networking with fellow Catholics and the potential obstacles, so what comes next? Networking must be a priority. Rethink your calendar. Be selfless and help others. Make personal interaction the ultimate goal versus simply connecting via the Internet. Vibrant networks take time to build and require a long-term commitment to sustain and grow them. Here are five practical ways to make a meaningful investment in networking:

1. Take an honest look at your calendar.

You may see little time for networking, but let me challenge you a bit. There are five opportunities a week for coffee/breakfast and five opportunities a week for lunch. Start using at least one of these times to schedule a weekly meeting with someone new. You have to eat, so you accomplish two tasks with the effort of one. Family time is vitally important, but perhaps a meeting a month at night may also be doable.

2. Make time for existing contacts in your network, both in and out of your organization.

Nurture these relationships at the same time you are expanding new ones. Also, ask these people for introductions to new contacts to build a larger, more relevant network. You likely already know some fellow Catholics. Spend more time with them and expand from there.

3. Popular business-networking Web sites are excellent tools for connecting with other Catholic professionals.

It is important to have complete and transparent profiles with pictures, but don't use these tools passively. There are recommendations for helpful groups you can join in Appendix 1. Popular social media network sites are also valuable tools, but for the Catholic professional, I suggest business networking sites.

4. Attend relevant speaker events, workshops, seminars, or other social mixers to meet fellow Catholic professionals.

I only attend these in the evening if I am hosting one of the monthly meetings of my parish business association ministry. There are ample opportunities for breakfast or lunchtime meetings. Consider hosting or cohosting events on your own. Organizing breakfast or lunch meetings with notable speakers on relevant topics allows you to play host and invite other Catholic business leaders you might not meet in other ways.

5. Volunteer and get involved in your parish community or your diocese.

Where is your passion? What causes excite you? Getting involved, first and foremost, should be about helping others. But volunteering your time and/or serving on nonprofit boards are excellent ways to meet like-minded professionals in the Catholic community.

It is important to integrate networking into other activities. Neighborhood swim meets, youth sports events, church social activities, and community volunteering all can be fortuitous opportunities to meet other professionals. I have found more success in these casual settings than through any other avenue. There is something authentic about connecting initially as parents, through shared interests and shared faith before discussing professional backgrounds. It builds trust that often leads to a mutually beneficial relationship.

WHERE CAN I GO? WHAT CAN I DO?

Over the years, I have either cofounded or become involved with a number of ministries and groups that actively facilitate connecting and networking for Catholics in the business community. Some are focused on inspiring Catholic speakers, others provide opportunities to share experiences as Catholic leaders in a confidential setting, and some offer networking opportunities in a more social environment. All of these provide wonderful opportunities to expand and grow in our knowledge of the faith, connect with new people on a personal level, and see examples of the impact Christ has had in the lives of others. You can find information for all of the following groups in Appendix 1:

1. Catholic business and professional clubs that typically feature breakfast programs and guest speakers who help you close the gap between your faith and your work.

2. The Young Catholic Professionals Group in Dallas, Texas. This group provides outstanding speakers and networking for young adult Catholics in the Dallas/Fort Worth area.

3. Parish-based jobs ministries, Catholic prayer meetings, and men's and women's club meetings in your parish are also great ways to meet fellow Catholics. Check out your Diocesan or Archdiocesan Web site as well as your own parish Web site for information on available groups in your area.

4. There are countless opportunities available that are only an Internet search away. *The Catholic Briefcase* would be a good resource and discussion book in these types of groups.

To conclude, I believe that Catholic business people who neglect their networks are missing out on a wonderful opportunity to tap into a supportive community, grow in their faith, and pay it forward. I have long told the stories of countless encounters with people I have met through my business who turned out to be Catholic and revealed their "secret identity" only after I first shared a little about me and my faith. As Catholics in the business community, we have too much to offer one another and the world to stay isolated in the vacuum of fear and apathy that seems to grip many in the Church today.

REFLECTION AND DISCUSSION

- Do I know other Catholic business people? Do I see value in knowing and interacting with them? What can I do to improve my efforts to connect with others in the Catholic business community?
- Do I know someone in the Catholic community who has been in career transition (see Appendix 3)? Would access to a community of people with my values be helpful during career transition? Why? Why not?

- Reflect on the quality of my networking and connections. Can it be improved? Commit to having one cup of coffee or lunch each week with a new person for the next month. At the end of this period, reflect on new ideas that have been learned, friendships that have begun, and review opportunities for sharing our Catholic faith. Consider if these were positive or negative experiences. What is my commitment to be more "connected" in the future?
- Would I consider starting a Catholic Business Group with other interested Catholics in my parish and community (see Appendix 4)?

CHAPTER 10

Signs of Our Faith

> *My fear of saying a simple blessing is a clear reminder to me that I don't have the courage to share my faith outside of my comfort zone.*

I RECALL A LUNCH I had with one of my new clients, a senior human resources executive of a sizable national company. Our working partnership had been very business-focused since the beginning, and I wanted to forge the kind of stronger personal connection that I enjoy with most of my other clients. We made small talk about a number of subjects until our food arrived. I said I was going to say a blessing over our meal and she was welcome to join me. As I made the sign of the cross and started to pray, I noticed that she also made the sign of the cross. I smiled to myself and said a quiet prayer of thanks for the opening I had been given.

Between bites of salad, I asked her which parish she attended. She gave me a funny look before responding with the name, then added, "that's a long story." I told her I would love to hear it, and for the next half-hour we talked about her faith journey, how much she loved her parish, her devotion to the Blessed Mother, and her prayer life. The awkward business-focused exchange at the beginning of the meal had been replaced by a warm conversation about our shared Catholic faith. I certainly achieved my goal of a stronger personal connection.

As we were preparing to leave, she shared that she never spoke of her faith in business settings and really enjoyed our discussion. As we were leaving the restaurant, we speculated on why Catholics don't discuss faith as openly as perhaps our Protestant brethren do. I suggested it may be fear of persecution or lack of confidence in defending the teachings of the Church. She suggested that it all came down to simple courage. I asked her to explain. Her response was, "When you made the sign of the cross in a crowded restaurant and said the blessing for all to hear, I realized that I never do that. My fear of saying a simple blessing is a clear reminder to me that I don't have the courage to share my faith outside of my comfort zone. I am grateful that you don't have that issue and also for this wonderful conversation."

Driving back to my office, I reflected on countless other business meals over the last few years that had turned into faith discussions, perhaps because of the simple act of making the sign of the cross and blessing the meal. I don't know whether I see this as courageous as much as following the call of Christ and the teachings of our Church. It is certainly food for thought and worthy of careful reflection.

What would happen if everyone who reads this makes a simple commitment to make the sign of the cross and say a blessing over every meal from now on, regardless of our companions? How many incredible faith discussions would happen as a result of this simple and public act of faith? I could easily argue the other side and share the possible negative outcomes, but can we live as faithful Catholics if we are paralyzed by fear? The answer, I believe, is that it is not only our duty, but our privilege to acknowledge Jesus and our faith. Through these small gestures that show our faith to others, we are fulfilling our promise to God to be disciples of his word and showing him our love as he calls us to do. Were we to live in fear of showing our love, it would not only weaken our faith but also make us more susceptible to steering away from God. Demonstrating your faith does not require you to make grandiose gestures, but merely a simple acknowledgment, or reminder, will help to keep your faith strong and abiding.

The sign of the cross in this business lunch example is a clear and obvious sign of our Catholic faith. What about others? The sacraments are visible signs of invisible grace instituted by Jesus Christ for our sanctification. The crucifix, saints, rosary, scapular, miracles, ashes on one's forehead on Ash Wednesday, etc., also are clear signs. As we consider the signs of our faith in the workplace, we need to realize that our actions and our behavior are being observed by those around us. For many, the first "signs" that we are Catholics may be visible in how we treat our coworkers, the way we make decisions, how we spend our time, or how we give back to the community. In the interest of upholding the practical theme of this book, let's examine the most effective signs of our faith, revealed in our willingness to show courage, humility, devotion, and joy in the workplace:

COURAGE

Being courageous about integrating our Catholic faith with our work can take many forms. The example of my lunch meeting and the sign of the cross was construed by my client as an act of courage. Consider the courage we can demonstrate by consistently doing the right thing at work and choosing good moral and ethical options in the face of judgment and criticism from others. Our willingness to place the needs of people before the bottom line is an act of courage sorely needed in business today. Finally, demonstrating simple bravery in sharing our faith with others at opportune moments can be the inspiration for them to join the Catholic Church and begin their journey to heaven.

HUMILITY

Humility is the virtue that overcomes the sin of pride. We all struggle with being prideful, especially in the workplace. Taking credit for our successes and working for self-satisfaction instead of giving glory to God is a clear example of pride. Perhaps a more insidious problem I have often observed is that of false humility. Recall the Scripture passage in Luke's Gospel about the Pharisee and the tax collector (Luke 18:9–14). The Pharisee looked with disdain on the tax collector as the man humbly declared his unworthiness and begged for forgiveness during his prayer. The Pharisee, on the other hand, was more concerned with boasting of his virtue and piety, and how he looked to others. He lacked humility and self-awareness. The tax collector's example is the better one to follow. God knows of our good deeds, and that is what matters. There's no need to brag to others. We can set a much better example if we are humble and ask our Lord for guidance and strength as we acknowledge our inadequacies.

PIETY

Being pious in the practice of our Catholic faith can make a great impression on others. While we want to avoid the poor example of the Pharisee, being open and humble in the practice of our faith can be the foundation for conversation with others who observe what we are doing. Consider committing an hour to eucharistic adoration each week (see Appendix 5). Attend daily Mass when possible. Go to frequent reconciliation. Set aside time for prayer each day. These acts of devotion are clear signs of our faith that keep us on the right path, while potentially providing inspiration to others.

JOY

I would argue that joy is the most profound sign of our faith we can exhibit to others in the workplace. Joy violates no company policies. Joy is contagious. Joy is a welcoming invitation to others.

The first Christians had the good fortune to be the first to share the Good News. Imagine the joy they felt in sharing Christ's message of love to everyone. They stood out as happy in a suffering world, just as Christians have an opportunity to do today. Jesus promised them (and us) this joy at the Last Supper when he said: "So you also are now in anguish. But I will see you again, and your hearts will rejoice, and no one will take your joy away from you" (John 16:22). Do we reflect joy at home, at work, and with friends? We have so much to be thankful for in our relationship with Christ. Being joyful should lead to sharing that joy with others and a willingness to express the truths of our faith in a way that shows the depth of our belief and love.

WHAT'S IN YOUR CATHOLIC BRIEFCASE?

As we try to show courage, humility, piety, and joy as signs of our Catholic faith, there are tools for those of us who need to make significant, heartfelt changes immediately. We can determine the tools we need by answering these questions:

- Do I make the sign of the cross and say a blessing over all my meals, regardless of my companions?
- Do I wish people "Merry Christmas" or "happy holidays/season's greetings?"
- Can people clearly see Christ at work in me?
- Do I show joy to others?
- Do I look for Christ in others?
- Do I attend daily Mass as often as possible?
- Do I go to frequent reconciliation?
- Do I observe all holy days and always attend Sunday Mass?
- Am I willing to be unpopular for taking stands in defense of Christ's teachings?
- Do I share the beauty and truth of my Catholic faith with others?
- Do I show excessive pride over my achievements, or am I humble and give the glory to God?
- Do I serve others with love and compassion?
- Do I set a good example for others in how I practice my Catholic faith?
- Do I truly place God first in all things, or is he merely contending for a piece of my time each day?

As we ponder the list, we should also consider the obstacles that impede our desire to integrate our lives and demonstrate the signs of faith outlined in this chapter. We allow fear, lukewarmness, greed, pride, and a host of other negative influences to affect how we think and act regarding our Catholic faith and our relationship with Jesus. The opinions of others often mean more to us than our relationship with him.

Saint Paul tells us that we should "rejoice always. Pray without ceasing. In all circumstances give thanks, for this is the will of God for you in Christ Jesus" (1 Thessalonians 5:16–18). He makes it sound so simple. Then why do we struggle to do something that is easy and that we should want to do anyway? We all deal with various forms of adversity. Some of us are unemployed, some are dealing with illness, and still others are struggling with a death in the family. The sex abuse crisis and the unwarranted attacks on Pope Benedict and the Church have made many Catholics gloomy and frightened. These are real obstacles to our faith that should be acknowledged.

The Church needs us to overcome these obstacles and live out our faith in the midst of the world. It is our obligation and our duty. The workplace is where we will spend the majority of our adult lives, and we can't exclude this vital arena from the practice of our faith. Remember, we are not alone. Be encouraged by this declaration: "I have the strength for everything through him who empowers me" (Philippians 4:13).

Our faith in Christ, our courage, our humility, our piety, and our heartfelt joy will see us through difficult times so we may be a good example for others. What kind of example are you setting for others today? What signs of our faith do others see in you? What will you do differently tomorrow?

REFLECTION AND DISCUSSION

- Have I had opportunities, such as the one the author had with the client over lunch, to make the sign of the cross? If so, how did I respond to those opportunities to say a blessing over the meal? After reflecting on this chapter, how might I act differently in the future?
- Of all the possible signs of faith, Christ-inspired joy can often have the most impact on others. What are the obstacles, if any, to me being joyful about my Catholic faith? What can I do to eliminate these obstacles?
- When I finished answering the list of questions in this chapter, did I see room for improvement? Make a list for future reflection on possible improvements and consider sharing it with accountability partners.
- Do I think first of the opinions of others in the public practice of my Catholic faith? Why? Do I fear judgment? Criticism? Is it possible that this could be an opportunity to explain my faith to others?

CHAPTER 11

It's Your Job, Not Your Vocation

> *You may be in the same room*
> *with your loved ones,*
> *but you must be present as well.*

FOR MANY OF US, it is all too common to put our jobs before God and our loved ones. As a recovering workaholic, I will admit that there were many years before my conversion to the Catholic Church that I placed my career first. I struggled with balance and easily justified my actions with excuses such as: "I'm the breadwinner," and "It's all for them." My family was serving my career instead of my career serving my family. An even bigger tragedy in those long years before my conversion is that God and faith did not play a role in my life. We become so focused on succeeding in our jobs that we often forget what we are working for in the first place. It is important to recognize this early on, as I can say from experience, because the more we put off our faith and God, the harder it is to realize what he does in our lives.

As I mentioned earlier, my wife and I joined the Catholic Church in the fall of 2005. I went through a profound personal conversion during the second Mass I ever attended. The culmination of years of work/life imbalance, no faith, and the challenges of "doing it my way" forced me to a point of feeling rudderless and overwhelmed. I was utterly lost. The real challenge was finally recognizing that I wasn't in charge of my life anymore. During those brief minutes I remember saying in my head, "I surrender!" And, "Christ, please lead me. I don't know what to do." I had never thought or said those words before, and as soon as I did, I felt an immediate sense of relief. I let go of over two decades of ego, arrogance, and pride.

I recognized in the days that followed that the Holy Spirit had gotten my attention in that Mass and my life priorities had to change. That was the beginning of a new chapter for me. I finally began placing Christ first in my life as I went through RCIA and came into the Church the next year with the rest of my family. Family comes second, and we all serve Christ together now. Work now ranks third…and my career has never been better!

There are many other stories and examples to consider. One is from Andy Mangione. Andy is the father of two sons, and, along with his wife, Amy, resides in Louisville, Kentucky. He has worked in sales for major companies, including Pfizer and Novartis, and is currently a sales executive for a large benefits provider where he works on one of the distribution channels. Andy is actively involved in his parish as a lector and religious education instructor. He also participates in a men's prayer group and the Knights of Columbus. Additionally, Andy hosts a weekly radio program on Louisville's Catholic radio station WLCR 1040 AM. The show, "His Father's Apprentice," focuses on Catholic fathers raising their sons to be honorable men of God.

Andy had me on his show not long ago, and I asked whether I could interview him for this book. His answers, advice, and the example he tries to set every day exemplify the essence of this chapter:

Q. How does putting Christ first, family second, and work third play out in your life?

A. Jesus Christ is the ultimate perspective-setter. Placing myself within the holy sacraments has made the priority of my earthly duties obvious to me. As fathers, we are blessed and commanded to lead our families to Christ and through him to his Father. That is our job. You can't be successful in this endeavor without nurturing and deepening your faith. Join a fellowship group at your parish. Let your children see you sacrificing and serving others outside the workplace. Attend Mass more than once a week. Above all, PRAY every day. Recognize the place in your life for work. As fathers, we must provide for our families. But don't let it (or any other distraction, like sports) interfere with your relationship with the Lord. Work hard and let your children witness your perseverance on work goals, but not at the expense of your relationship with your family. All of this is a daily focus and struggle for me, but my family and our journey to heaven is more important than any job.

Q. What are practical ways you can make your family your true vocation?

A. Take an active role in your children's Catholic formation. The majority of our children's formation is supposed to take place within the home. Also, work on your own formation. Attend Bible study. Read apologetics so you may clearly explain the sacraments, Mass, and other important aspects of our wonderful Catholic faith to your children. Don't think that sending your child to a Catholic or Christian school ends your responsibility regarding their formation.

These schools merely augment the effort that should be taking place at home. Realize that your priority in life is to lead your family to Christ and ultimately his Father's kingdom through a solid foundation of faith. Make your parish a second home for your children. Let them get to know the children of fellow parishioners. Include your parish as an activity center for your children. But all of this requires a time commitment on your part. Are you willing to walk away from work at a decent hour to join the family for dinner? Can you put down the BlackBerry or iPhone when you are home to engage with the family?

Q. What are the obstacles to making this a reality?

A. Popular culture is a huge obstacle. The Internet and prime-time television assault Christian morals and ideals on a nonstop basis. Television alone perpetuates a distorted image of the family in general and fatherhood in particular. Severely restrict what you allow to enter your home and work hard to ensure that your home is not defiled by the secular culture. Don't allow television or electronic games to be the chief occupiers of your children's time. Make sure the quality of your time with loved ones is a priority. You may be in the same room with your loved ones, but you must be present as well.

Q. Has your business career suffered from this focus?

A. No. By recognizing Christ in everyone I encounter, including those at work, my ego and I are taken out of the equation. I find it easier (and more peaceful) to deal with a "difficult" colleague through the eyes of Christ rather than my own. This also places work in the proper perspective for me. My boss is Jesus Christ, not a mortal man or woman. Also, do not be afraid to place a prayer or rosary in your office or cubicle. Witness your faith at work. If people ask why you have ashes on your forehead on Ash Wednesday, engage them and tell them why.

Q. What advice do you have for single Catholics in the workplace around this idea of career versus vocation?

A. You can't have success without first having a relationship with God. Everything flows through Christ. Jesus is responsible for us taking our next breath, not just winning that coveted promotion. If you are eventually called to become a husband, wife, father, or mother, the strong faith you establish as a single adult will make an integrated life in the service of Christ much more likely.

Andy has chosen to be transparent about what he believes and joyful about living out his faith. There is much we can learn from his example. Which obstacles get in the way of us putting Christ, the pursuit of heaven, and our families before our work? Andy identified popular culture as the main culprit, and I would add that our society's addiction to materialism is also a significant challenge. I agree that popular culture, as represented by the media and retail advertisers, has invaded virtually every electronic gadget or print product we own, use, or see every day. We have been sold for decades on the idea of a lifestyle filled with fun, convenience, and, dare I say, guilt if we don't pursue this artificial paradise. The push is to buy, buy, buy, and then buy some more.

The focus on acquiring material goods drives many of us to work harder and harder to make more money to buy bigger houses, nicer cars, and cooler gadgets. This obsession often pulls both parents into the work force to support their lifestyle, keep up with the neighbors, or satisfy some deep inner emptiness. There is nothing wrong with a nice lifestyle, but how much is enough? And more important, at the end of our lives, can we take it with us? Our Lord said: "Do not store up for yourselves treasures on earth, where moth and decay destroy, and thieves break in and steal. But store up treasures in heaven, where neither moth nor decay destroys, nor thieves break in and steal. For where your treasure is, there also will your heart be" (Matthew 6:19–21). This clear direction from Jesus means we need to take better inventory of our lives. We need to make sure that God is not just one of our priorities, but instead he must be the top priority. As Jesus said: "No one can serve two masters. He will either hate one and love the other, or be devoted to one and despise the other. You cannot serve God and mammon. But seek first the kingdom (of God) and his righteousness, and all these things will be given you besides. Do not worry about tomorrow; tomorrow will take care of itself..." (Matthew 6:24, 33–34).

Please don't misunderstand me: supporting our families comfortably is not in itself wrong. I am talking about the excessive and disordered attachment to material goods that takes our focus away from Christ and our faith journey. Just think about the key words we place before the material things we desire during the course of a day: "I want," "I need," or "I love." Now, replace these material things with God and use the same key words. We should all want, need, and love God, and our thoughts should always be of him.

Even though I have focused primarily on the obstacles presented by materialism, please also recognize how we can create false gods out of our work or the pursuit of pleasure (drugs, gambling, sex, sports, hobbies, etc.). Any object, activity, or feeling that has our excessive, disordered attachment and devotion comes between us and our heavenly Father and is, in effect, a surrogate god. What if we challenge ourselves to be good stewards of our gifts and abundance? Consider the impact on our relationship with God and our community as well as the inspiration our children will receive if we place more emphasis on charitable giving than on acquiring things we don't need.

Time on earth with our families is precious, and we will be remembered and judged by how well we live that time. Achieving quality time with our loved ones requires living in the moment, avoiding distractions from work, appreciating the gift of our families, and being the loving parent or spouse that God intends us to be. Here are some ideas to consider:

SPEND TIME WITH OUR LOVED ONES, NOT MONEY

Our children require our time, love, guidance, and boundaries. In the absence of a positive alternative, television, computers, and video games are swiftly becoming the modern world's surrogate parents and are teaching our kids that materialism is a god worth following. It is our responsibility to show them otherwise, so let's put away our wallets and invest quality time in those we love.

SET A GOOD FAITH EXAMPLE FOR OUR CHILDREN

If you want to know what kind of Catholics our children will be, look in the mirror. They look to Mom and Dad and mimic our example. If we pray, they will pray. If we are joyful about attending Mass, they will be excited as well. Discuss Scripture and Bible stories. Point out appropriate heroes for them among the figures of the Bible or saints who have lived exemplary lives.

THE FAMILY THAT PRAYS TOGETHER STAYS TOGETHER

Like many of you, this is a challenge my family faces. We pray before mealtime and bedtime with our children, and I hope the meaning of what we are doing will sink in. But raising children is a marathon, not a sprint. Let's keep at it, and eventually we will reach them.

WE ARE HERE TO HELP OUR FAMILIES
(AND EVERYONE ELSE) GET TO HEAVEN

As parents, we have no greater responsibility than to help our families get to heaven. It is our mission and our vocation. As part of leading an integrated life, we should always consider how to bring our children, our loved ones, and everyone else closer to Christ and our goal of heaven. As Andy Mangione shared, it is not a school's or the Church's responsibility to develop our children's faith—it is ours.

As a Catholic husband, father, and business leader with a young family, I am worried about the future for my children and the world they will inherit. But I am comforted by the knowledge that Jesus gave us the gift of his Church, a teacher whose purpose is to help my family and me follow his teachings and get to heaven. I struggle with the same challenges as many of you, and I don't pretend to have all the answers. I do know that it is not too late to turn away from the things of this world and place our relationship with God and our children on a proper footing.

As you ponder this chapter, please reflect on this powerful insight from Deacon Mike Bickerstaff: "God has created us for a purpose, a supernatural end. We are to come to know, love, and serve him in this life and spend a joyful eternity in communion with him in the life to come. This call to holiness is our vocation. We live this vocation as clergy, religious or laity, married or single. Nothing we do is more important than attaining this end. Therefore, we must avoid anything that harms or impedes our vocation. Every moment given to us by God—whether spent at home, in the office, or in the marketplace—is a moment of grace to say 'yes' to God's call. Our life of faith is to be lived 24/7."

REFLECTION AND DISCUSSION

- Does my job serve Jesus and my family, or is it the other way around? What steps can I take to get my priorities in order?
- What influence does the secular world and popular culture have on my motivations for working and my lifestyle? Does this influence impact me in a negative way? Why? Reflect on what I might be missing in my life as a result of my attitude toward money and working.
- Reflect on what would happen if I go to work tomorrow with a firm commitment to place Christ first, family second, and work third on my list of priorities. How can I make this a reality?

CHAPTER 12

Start With
the End in Mind

*We have a heavenly
destination before us.*

AT THE 2010 Second Annual Atlanta Catholic Business Conference (which I cofounded in 2008), I gave a talk called "Being Catholic at Work." I identified the obstacles before us in living out our Catholic faith in the workplace and challenged the audience to "start with the end in mind." We have a heavenly destination before us. I can't think of a better motivation for practicing our Catholic faith in the workplace than this mental image: Picture Jesus greeting you in heaven with the words, "Well done, good and faithful servant." We have a lifetime, including our time at work, to love and serve the Lord. Will we use it wisely? What will Jesus say to us at the end of our lives?

As I considered Catholic business people to include in the book who clearly understood and lived this concept of working toward heaven, I immediately thought of Alex Muñoz. Alex was a featured speaker at the 2011 Annual Atlanta Catholic Business Conference and is a well-respected business leader, speaker, husband, and father. He owns CSR, LLC, a business services consulting firm that specializes in the startup or turnaround of small- to medium-sized organizations. He and his wife, María, have five children and are very active in their parish community. They are frequent speakers at marriage enrichment events and diocesan catechetical workshops.

There are many things about Alex that I admire, including his passion for the Catholic faith and his clarity in understanding the role that faith plays in the public square. I asked Alex for his insights into our journey toward heaven:

Q. What is our mission here on earth?

A. My mission is to know, love, and serve God and get myself, spouse, children, and as many people as possible to heaven. Along the way, God has placed situations and creatures ("creatures" = assets, tools, etc.) in my way that can help me become the person that he always had in mind for me to become. Much in the way the transfiguration revealed to us Jesus in all of his splendor and how he really is, we are similarly called to be what he wanted us to be like from the very beginning, before sin and concupiscence got in the way.

Having said all that, being blessed with material goods is a great way to move God's kingdom on earth forward as well as continue the process of sanctifying yourself. Few people who are benefactors of a charity or religious work are unchanged after their investment of time, talent, or treasure. Now, accumulating wealth for the express reason of accumulating it calls to mind the parable of the rich man in the Gospels: "Someone in the crowd said to him, 'Teacher, tell my brother to share the inheritance with me.' He replied to him, 'Friend, who appointed me as your judge and arbitrator?' Then he said to the crowd, 'Take care to guard against all greed, for though one may be rich, one's life does not consist of possessions.' Then he told them a parable: 'There was a rich man whose land produced a bountiful harvest. He asked himself, "What shall I do, for I do not have space to store my harvest?" And he said, "This is what I shall do: I shall tear down my barns and build larger ones. There I shall store all my grain and other goods and I shall say to myself, 'Now as for you, you have so many good things stored up for many years, rest, eat, drink, be merry!'" But God said to him, 'You fool! This night your life will be demanded of you; and the things you have prepared, to whom will they belong?' Thus will it be for the one who stores up treasure for himself but is not rich in what matters to God'" (Luke 12:13–21). Wealth is neither good nor bad—it's how it's used that is important.

Q. How does getting to heaven fit with the modern view of work?

A. The way I make it fit is one that resonates with many folks who are wired the same way I am—that is, if you are a believer and are also seeking excellence in your life, you have no other approach other than to be the best in everything that you do, including and especially your faith life. One has to be careful here, though, and not fall into the compartmentalization fallacy. What has helped me a lot is to consider faith and my relationship with God as a bookcase versus one of the volumes in the bookcase. Seeing my relationship with God as the overall encompassing vehicle in my life ensures that I have integrity in everything that I do, including my work. Work becomes another activity that I can do to show God how much I love and trust him. It is another expression of my fidelity and gratitude for everything in my life as much as being a good husband and father is and can be. The difficulties with work become little gifts I can make to him of how deeply I trust him; the decision to deepen my knowledge of the faith and my relationship with him is an expression of how I want to have balance in my life and be as educated and professional in my faith as I am with my education and work.

Q. *How would you encourage Catholics reading this book to begin their own journeys?*

A. First, clearly recognize and understand that our final destination is heaven. I am called to get there and bring as many people as I can with me (starting with my wife and children). In my work, both as an employee as well as for the past almost nine years on my own, I have emphasized a common sense-oriented approach to resolving problems or leveraging opportunities. This is not an approach that is limited to the secular—I really believe that God wants us to not compartmentalize, but to integrate our faith in all parts of our life. As such, I have a very practical approach to my faith.

Continuing the analogy of a journey, I never leave home without first examining what I want to get done on my trip and where I need to go. Is it for business or pleasure? What type of climate will I be experiencing? What happens if the climate changes? Do I need to be prepared for those contingencies? What map am I bringing?

In the spiritual life, it's much the same. What has formed me as the person I am today, and to which all success is attributed, is a close relationship with God. Every year since I was a teenager, I have had the grace to attend spiritual exercises. I guess the best way, business-wise, to think about this is as having your MBOs with God [Management by Objectives]. First, I map out beforehand the weekend (it typically starts on a Thursday or Friday night and goes through Sunday) that I am going to do this. Note: Satan, who is very real and exists, does not want you to attend these kinds of retreats. Though it may be obvious, let me belabor the point—every time you are in silence and give God the chance to speak to you,

HE WILL! A very wise Jesuit once shared with me that if you go every year to spiritual exercises, you can pluck out the weeds while they are still young and tender; they have only had the intervening year in which to grow in your garden. If you don't go each year (or do something similar to this), it gets much more difficult. In my mind's eye, I see a vast field of kudzu growing in the distance or a huge redwood tree. Definitely not the way to go.

Q. What are practical ways Catholics in the workplace can stay focused on the journey's end?

A. Like a business needs a plan to be successful, we need a plan to be successful Catholics (or at least to be organized in our approach to it). I think it's Stephen Covey who says that if the ladder is not leaning against the right wall, every step we take just gets us to the wrong place faster. As I said in my answer to your last question, I have been blessed to have been able to attend a silent retreat (the Spiritual Exercises of Saint Ignatius of Loyola) every year since I was in high school. In it, the retreat master takes the participants through guided meditations and a framework or "Program of Life" is developed. This is a plan that identifies one's weaknesses (vice) and the corresponding means to counteract/strengthen it (virtue).

With very practical steps (such as problem identification and development of a project plan using systems theory), one can take the human tools that God has allowed us to develop and apply them in the spiritual realm. Use of this plan is essential to drive activity levels both at home and work. In fact, specific struggles at work can be identified as areas of opportunity to target and work on so that the work environment can be addressed. Using the idea of all weaknesses being able to be broken down into three main vices (pride, vanity, and sensuality), the corresponding plan can be structured to address these shortcomings. Struggling with a boss who is making your life impossible because of micromanagement of your work? There are very specific tactics that you can implement to build and address that situation. But without the accompanying humility (that is, swallow your pride) and internal transformation on your part, little progress will be achieved.

In his presentation at the Atlanta Catholic Business Conference, Alex also shared some practical ideas on how to "pack your bags with common sense tools" for the journey before us. Here is a summary:

- **Overcommunicate.** Listen and lead. To paraphrase the quote attributed to Saint Francis, "Lead with words, only if necessary." Practice "charity is clarity" by asking the tough questions, use stories and analogies to make points and always speak with someone in person.
- **Pick travel companions with a purpose.** Surround yourself with friends, a loving and supportive spouse (if you are called to marriage as a vocation), and trusted business associates. Ask yourself: "Does the person bring you closer to or separate you from Christ?"
- **Pack your Bible and plan for the sacraments.** Make a plan you can stick with. The pilgrimage is a spiritual one that is ongoing and never ends in this life. Focus on a life of personal prayer, go to regular reconciliation and receive the Eucharist whenever possible.
- **Bring a compass to keep you traveling in the right direction— toward heaven.** Attend yearly spiritual retreats where you review your previous year. With the guidance and inspiration of the Holy Spirit, set concrete objectives/goals for the coming year.

Alex's ideas and the experiences he shared are clear, actionable, and achievable. The key to understanding his perspectives is realizing how seamlessly he has integrated his faith with his professional life. There is no distinction and certainly no compartmentalization. He has the goal of heaven for himself and everyone around him firmly planted in his mind. A successful journey always begins with knowing your destination.

In addition to recognizing heaven as our final destination, we must also realize that we are called to lead lives of holiness. John Paul II wrote in *Christifideles Laici*: "The call to holiness is rooted in Baptism and proposed anew in the other Sacraments, principally in the Eucharist. Since Christians are reclothed in Christ Jesus and refreshed by his Spirit, they are 'holy.' They therefore have the ability to manifest this holiness and the responsibility to bear witness to it in all that they do. The Apostle Paul never tires of admonishing all Christians to live 'as is fitting among saints' (Ephesians 5:3)."[14]

We can reflect carefully on these points to more clearly see how to conduct ourselves on our faith journeys (the call to holiness) toward our final destination (heaven). As Catholics, we are set apart. Therefore we do not allow ourselves to be assimilated into the surrounding culture. That requires courage, since trials and often loneliness are on this path, but we know what our final reward will be if we embrace our calling.

In my professional life I lead an executive recruiting firm and am also actively involved in ministry work focused on helping people integrate faith, family, and work. I am blessed through both of these channels to encounter hundreds of men and women every year and spend time with them discussing their lives, goals, and challenges. I have observed in many of these good people a consistent desire to achieve balance in their lives, be stronger in their faith, and be better stewards in the community.

What are the catalysts that create these desires? A large number of people I meet are in transition, looking for a new career. Many are business leaders who are burned out and frustrated by years of climbing the corporate ladder. Still others recognize that their families are serving their jobs, instead of the other way around. Some just recognize that they have little or no faith and they have done a poor job of using their God-given gifts and talents to serve others. Whatever the reason, I suggest that there is a growing desire to lead richer, fuller lives filled with balance, purpose, and meaning.

My hope is for everyone to undergo a true "conversion of the soul" and lead an integrated, balanced, and meaningful life. It isn't easy, but it's worth the journey. I encourage you to begin tomorrow with a firm disposition to do good, practice virtue, and emulate Christ. Thank God and praise his name. Pray throughout the day. Be kind to people you meet and offer assistance freely without an expectation of return. Ask Jesus in prayer to show you that the challenges that present themselves each day are opportunities to grow in holiness and virtue. Be a light for Christ to all you encounter and never forget that we are all made for heaven, not this place called earth, and the journey leads through the workplace.

REFLECTION AND DISCUSSION

- We are made for heaven and not this place. Do we spend our lives with the correct "end in mind?" Do my actions and thinking currently align with this idea?
- The road to heaven for many leads through the workplace. How will I work to ensure that the large portion of my life spent at work will help me on this journey?
- Alex Muñoz laid out very practical ideas and actions based on his life and experiences. Can I incorporate some of these into my life? Make an action plan that works for me, like Alex did, to keep the focus on getting myself and everyone else I know to heaven. Reflect on this plan and refer to it often.

CONCLUSION

A Call to Action

I HOPE EVERY CHAPTER you have read in this book offered some new ideas, perspectives, and practical tools for integrating your Catholic faith with your work. With so many different ideas to share on this important topic, this could have easily been a thirty-chapter book. My sincere hope is that—at a bare minimum—you will begin to view your job differently. Instead of a day focused on making a living, you can instead become focused on faith-based living throughout your day. In the career God gave specifically to you, he equipped you with specific talents and interests to serve him, others, and the Church. You are a critical piece in the puzzle of life and the body of Christ.

No matter whether we are called to the single or married life, if we are a teenager or near retirement, there are countless demands on our time each and every day. Our challenge is to think about how we spend that time. Does our job support our family, or does our family support our job? Carve out quiet time for reflection and leisure. Integrate prayer into our schedule. Offer up our workdays to God. Look at every encounter as a chance to serve others and show *agape* love. Reflect an attitude of joy to others. Make better decisions by running them through the filter of our Catholic faith. Be better stewards of the gifts God has given us. Set a better example for others. The suggestions in each chapter, quotes from the saints, writings of our popes, and the real examples and stories of Catholics just like you throughout the book are there to show the way.

The idea of integration may still be a little overwhelming, but believe me when I say it is simpler than you may think. It is OK to take baby steps on your journey. Begin by being more attentive to the needs of others and trying to give back selflessly to one person this week. That's a great start. In the following week, add the Jesuit Daily Examen to your calendar and enjoy these three- to five-minute periods of reflection in prayer (see Appendix 2). Look for ways to connect with the larger Catholic community—especially fellow business people—for encouragement, support, and ideas. Above all, let go of the erroneous notion that you must leave the most important part of who you are at the door of your office. Our workday, like everything else, belongs to God. We must remember to give up our work to God's greater glory and not make it the mere pursuit of our own self-satisfaction.

Of course, none of this matters if we are not serious about the practice of our Catholic faith. We can't practice at work what we are not living elsewhere. Going to Mass on Sundays and holy days is not enough. We are called to lead lives of holiness, and we are made for heaven. Perhaps we should look at integrating our Catholic faith with the workplace as the missing ingredient, the catalyst, to taking our Catholic faith to the next level. With commitment, courage, humility, and the guidance of the Holy Spirit, this can become a reality.

Are you ready to begin?

APPENDIX 1

Helpful Resources

Recommended Web Sites

Vatican: vatican.va
U.S. Conference of Catholic Bishops: usccb.org
EWTN: ewtn.com
Catholics Come Home: catholicscomehome.org
Catholic Business Journal: catholicbusinessjournal.biz
Integrated Catholic Life e-magazine: integratedcatholiclife.org

Recommended Groups on LinkedIn

Catholic Networkers
Catholic Professionals
Atlanta Catholic Business Conference
Heart of America Catholic Business Network
Catholic Business League
Catholic Business Owners
Legatus

Recommended Apps

iMissal
irosary

Confession: A Roman Catholic App
Catholic Calendar (Universalis Publishing)
Catholic News Live (CNL)
Catholic Quote of the Day

Organizations and Ministries

Saint Peter Chanel Business Association (Faith at Work)
stpeterchanel.org/adulted/speakersseries.html

Catholic Business Café
stpeterchanel.org/adulted/speakersseries.html

Annual Atlanta Catholic Business Conference
integratedcatholiclife.org/acbc/

Woodstock Business Conference
woodstock.georgetown.edu/programs/woodstock-
business-conference.html

Young Catholic Professionals Group
facebook.com/youngcatholicprofessionals

Catholics@Work
catholicsatwork.org

Catholic Business Network
catholicbusinessnetwork.net

The Catholic Business Professionals of Greater Philadelphia
catholicpros.com

Catholic Business League
catholicbusinessleague.org

Legatus
legatus.org

Recommended Reading

In Conversation With God, by Francis Fernandez (Sceptre London, 2005)

The Spiritual Exercises of Saint Ignatius of Loyola, by Saint Ignatius of Loyola (TAN Books, 1914)

Deep Conversion, Deep Prayer, by Father Thomas Dubay (Ignatius Press, 2006)

Living the Catholic Faith: Rediscovering the Basics, by Archbishop Charles Chaput (Charis Books, 2001)

He Leadeth Me, by Father Walter J. Ciszek, SJ (Ignatius Press, 1995)

The Virtue Driven Life, by Father Benedict J. Groeschel (Our Sunday Visitor, 2006)

Heroic Leadership: Best Practices From a 450-Year-Old Company That Changed the World, by Chris Lowney (Loyola Press, 2003)

Prayer in the Digital Age, by Matt Swaim (Liguori Publications, 2011)

Doing the Right Thing at Work: A Catholic's Guide to Faith, Ethics and Business, by James L. Nolan (St. Anthony Messenger Press, 2005)

Back to Virtue, by Peter Kreeft (Ignatius Press, 1992)

Five Pillars of the Spiritual Life: A Practical Guide to Prayer for Active People, by Father Robert Spitzer (Ignatius Press, 2008)

Jesus-Shock, by Peter Kreeft (St. Augustine's Press, 2008)

Mere Christianity, by C.S. Lewis (Harper San Francisco, 2001)

Rich Where It Counts: Create Lasting Wealth by Cultivating Spiritual Capital, by Charles V. Douglas (Morgan James Publishing, 2006)

Business as a Calling: Work and the Examined Life, by Michael Novak (Free Press, 1996)

Bringing Your Business to Life: The Four Virtues That Will Help You Build a Better Business and a Better Life, by Jeffrey Cornwall and Michael Naughton (Regal, 2008)

Recommended Papal and Church Documents

Christifideles Laici: Blessed John Paul II

Centisimus Annus: Blessed John Paul II

Fides et Ratio: Blessed John Paul II

Laborem Exercens: Blessed John Paul II

Caritas in Veritate: Pope Benedict XVI

Pastoral Constitution on the Church in the Modern World (*Gaudium et Spes*): Second Vatican Council

A Catholic Framework for Economic Life: A Statement of the U.S. Catholic Bishops

APPENDIX 2

Daily Examen for Busy Business People

Adapted by Martin J. O'Malley, SJ, from *The Spiritual Exercises of Saint Ignatius of Loyola*.

Thanksgiving

Begin by relaxing into God's presence in an attitude of thankfulness. Find one thing to be thankful for, even if you are having a tough time. Allow gratitude to take hold of you.

Pray for Insight

Pray to the Holy Spirit to reveal to you what you need at this time. Consciously open yourself to God's light.

Finding God in All Things

This is the heart of the prayer, where you examine very concretely the events of the day.

—What happened since this morning?
—Whom have you come in contact with?
—What occupies your thoughts today?
—How are you being drawn to God in your life today? Now?

—Where is God calling you specifically this day?

—Is it time to make a tough decision that will affect the lives of many people?

—Should I simply bask in gratefulness to God for my life, career, and family?

This is not a time for searching for faults. Rather, it is a chance to take a step back and recognize that God is active in the entirety of the day.

Petition

Express to God your desires. Be specific and frame your prayer here in a petition: "Dear Lord, at this time I ask...for strength to... for courage to...for the resolve to...to be thankful for..."

Resolve for the Future

Finally, look to the future. "How shall I live the rest of the day?" "What shall I do?"

Finish with a prayer, for example, the Our Father.

These excerpts from *The Spiritual Exercises of Saint Ignatius of Loyola* were taken from *Doing the Right Thing at Work: A Catholic's Guide to Faith, Business and Ethics*, by James L. Nolan (Cincinnati: St. Anthony Messenger Press, 2005), and are used by permission. All rights reserved.

Job Seekers Should Expect More From Us

YOU MAY find it odd to read about helping job seekers in a book about integrating faith and work, but this ties in with much of what you have read about stewardship, serving others, *agape* love, and connecting with a community. With so many people in career transition over the last few years because of the challenging economic climate, chances are that you or someone you know have been in the ranks of the unemployed for a period of time.

I recently had an epiphany related to people in career transition. I have been counseling job seekers for many years and have written several articles on job search strategy. My epiphany (or firm grasp of the obvious?) is that I rarely read or hear any meaningful instruction on how we are supposed to help people in transition. The interview coaching, résumé writing, networking, social media, psychology of job search articles abound, but there is very little helpful information or guidance on what you and I can do to help job seekers.

This is an important topic. With a high unemployment rate, it is likely that we all know friends and family affected by this tough economy. It may be difficult to admit, but at some point we run out of helpful advice. We may even start to avoid these wonderful people who need our assistance because we feel embarrassed that we don't know what to do or how to help. What is the solution?

I suggest that we consider five areas in which we can make a significant and realistic impact. What may surprise you is how basic these ideas are, and yet I rarely observe them being used effectively. For your consideration:

1. Pray.

Prayer will be the most powerful assistance we can provide if we are sincere and consistent in asking for the help and guidance of the Holy Spirit to assist those in need of work. Pray to Saint Joseph, the Patron Saint of Workers, and ask for his intercession for those seeking employment. Ask the Blessed Mother for her intercession and help. She will never deny those who seek her assistance.

2. Be active listeners.

When someone needs our help, we need to understand all the facts. We need to know how she or he is handling the situation. Too often we may have a tendency to launch into offering solutions before we have a full understanding of the issues. Sometimes those who seek our help just need to vent or be heard. Let's listen.

3. Be candid.

I have had countless job seekers tell me how much they appreciate my sharing honest and tough feedback with them. What is surprising is that they had not heard this information from others in their circle. It is in our nature to avoid hurting someone's feelings, but we are doing more damage than we can imagine by not sharing the truth. Poorly written résumés, incomplete business networking profiles, poor "elevator pitches," an inability to answer questions about their backgrounds, and lack of follow-up are just a few examples of the many forms of candid feedback we should share if warranted. We are doing more harm than good by saying everything is great and they are right on track, if, in fact, they aren't.

4. Be encouraging.

Encouragement is the NOT the opposite of candor. I meant every word I wrote in the third point about sharing the difficult truth, but we also need to be encouraging to those in career transition. It is a very tough situation for anyone. Just consider for a moment how we would feel if the roles were reversed. Empathy, understanding, and positive reinforcement are always appreciated.

I don't want to overexplain something as basic as encouragement, but one helpful aspect of encouragement we may fail to consider is inclusion. Don't overlook inviting people in career transition to business-related events or other gatherings. Job seekers often tell me how alienated they feel, and that they want to retreat from the world, especially in the first months after a job loss. If we want to truly encourage and help, let's help them stay plugged in to our networks where they can make useful contacts and feel connected to the world to which they are longing to return. It also would be great for us to have an occasional coffee or lunch meeting to touch base when our schedules allow.

5. Act immediately.

Based on my experience and feedback from others, we often have conversations with job seekers and think of multiple referrals we can make to useful contacts in our network. Ideas for help on multiple fronts may be discussed, and the meeting concludes on a very positive note. We get back to our offices or homes and other priorities pop up, and we are consumed by our own challenges. Days or weeks go by and we have forgotten to follow up, leaving the job seeker frustrated and wondering why he met with us in the first place. Remember that job seekers are racing the clock. The financial, emotional, and mental pressures are mounting daily for them.

Here is a helpful checklist to make your interactions with job seekers more meaningful:

- Ask the job seeker to invite you to join his business Internet network and get back to you if he sees useful contacts.
- Challenge the job seeker to develop a target list of specific companies he is interested in and ask him to e-mail you this information.
- Ask the job seeker to send you a short e-mail recapping the meeting, with his résumé attached. Let him know that you will be forwarding that e-mail to people in your network with a recommendation for a meeting. Here is an example of what his e-mail to you should look like:

> Bill,
>
> Thank you for meeting with me today. I really enjoyed our conversation and appreciate your willingness to help me grow my network. As we discussed, I am looking for a senior sales leadership role in a growing technology company. I have a long track record of success in my past roles and will bring leadership experience, a great reputation, and a wealth of contacts to a new position. Again, I am grateful for your assistance, and I look forward to speaking with you again soon.
>
> Sincerely,
> Mike Smith

- Ask the job seeker to follow up with you on any action items in your discussion as well as to keep you updated on the progress of his search. Be mindful of your personal workload and don't over-commit, but an e-mail every two weeks is probably appropriate.
- Pull out your smartphone in the meeting and share phone numbers and e-mail addresses of helpful contacts with the job seeker. Why wait? Have him reach out directly, copy you on any e-mails, and you have just saved a huge follow-up step.

Did you notice that in most of the examples I gave, the job seeker is given a specific follow-up item? This is important because you are asking this individual to help you, so help him. This approach is more efficient, contains more accountability and ultimately gets the job seeker what he needs from us—warm contacts.

I could write a book on this subject, as there are so many ways we could assist our friends, family, and professional network in their search for employment. My goal is to keep it simple and share with you the benefit of countless conversations I have had with people in career transition and my observations about the struggles we all have to help these good people achieve their goal of regaining employment. Remember the Golden Rule, prayers are always helpful, and reflect on this powerful quote (attributed to many): "There, but for the grace of God, go I."

APPENDIX 4

Road Map for Building a Catholic Business Group

IT ALL STARTED with an Internet search. In the spring of 2007, I was seeking a new book to recommend in the monthly e-newsletter put out by a ministry I lead called the Saint Peter Chanel Business Association. My search was for a book on integrating faith and work, and Jim Nolan's *Doing the Right Thing at Work: A Catholic's Guide to Faith, Ethics and Business* came up on the first results page. I bought the book and was intrigued by his case studies about Catholic business leaders and professionals working through ethical and moral issues in the workplace, as well as his approach through the Woodstock Business Conference to help members of the group integrate faith, family, and their professional lives.

I contacted Jim Nolan that summer and asked about starting an Atlanta chapter of the WBC. Jim's gracious counsel and assistance was the catalyst we needed to successfully launch the Atlanta chapter in August 2007. With Jim's help and the many resources he provided, we got off to a great start and have continued to thrive ever since. We currently have nineteen active members in our chapter and average fourteen to seventeen attendees at each meeting. We feel that God has truly blessed our efforts, and our chapter members have been transformed from a cautious exploration of integrating faith and work into the active practice of being lights for Christ in the workplace.

I have attempted to capture in this case study our approach to growing the Atlanta chapter. We don't pretend to have all the answers and still have much to learn, but we are excited and energized about the journey of discovery that lies ahead of us. What follows is a detailed look at how we have approached developing and growing our group.

The Meetings

Our monthly meetings occur the last Wednesday of every month right after 6:45 a.m. Mass, which all members are encouraged to attend. The meetings last from 7:15 to 8:30 a.m. and are the lifeblood of WBC Atlanta (and any chapter for that matter). We have kept the time and location of meetings very consistent for the benefit of our members. Continuity is a good thing. Our group members have frequently stated that they truly look forward to our meetings. This enthusiasm shows as they are usually well-prepared, have done their reading, and the discussions we have reveal a sincere depth of understanding for the topic(s). Here are several factors that we believe contribute to the success of our meetings:

Preparation—The group is supplied with the topic, Scripture, and supporting articles or other reading at least ten days in advance of the meeting. A reminder is usually sent two days out from the meeting. To some degree, peer pressure helps encourage people to be prepared, but I also believe the group genuinely wants to be ready for the discussions.

Guide the meeting, but don't be rigid—My job as coordinator is to present the topic and Scripture, facilitate a vibrant dialogue, and keep us on schedule. I have learned to let our conversations go a little off track if they are relevant and helpful. Sometimes our Scripture reflection dominates the discussion, and at other times the topic is the main focus. Flexibility is important as long as the meetings mostly stay on track.

Study and discuss relevant topics—I recommend that all new groups cover Jim Nolan's book in their first year. It was a great introduction into the WBC for us and got our group off to a good start. It is also important to use topics and resource materials that are relevant to your group and their interests, while still following the WBC process. For our third year as a chapter, we worked from Father Benedict J. Groeschel's book, *A Virtue Driven Life,* and Father Robert J. Spitzer's book, *The Five Pillars of the Spiritual Life: A Practical Guide to Prayer for Active People.* Our chapter had a strong desire to explore the practical application of virtue in their lives and to focus on building an interior life. These books support that goal and have been very well-received. *The Catholic Briefcase* would also be an excellent resource for this type of group discussion.

Keep it fresh—In our second year, we rotated back and forth between the two books listed above to add variety. Also, throughout the year, we will typically have a few white-board sessions (usually additional meetings) where we brainstorm our ideas on a white board and really dive into applying what we are learning in our professional lives. We also invite guests from time and have a retired priest who attends frequently. These objective voices add a lot to our discussions.

Inspire trust and open sharing—All opinions are valid, and we don't "shoot the messenger." We have always aimed for open and candid dialogue in our meetings, and we have largely achieved that because our group members absolutely trust each other.

One of the other important reasons for our successful meetings, which could be an article in itself, is our focus on diligent follow-up. Careful notes are taken of our meetings, and a recap of our discussion is shared within forty-eight hours of the meeting. This serves as a good source of reminders for the group, keeps a careful recording of our chapter's work for posterity, and helps us understand better what topics really resonated with our group as we consider future subjects.

Growing Our Chapter

We have a specific goal of adding at least one new person to our group each quarter. With work travel, job changes, and occasional moves, it is critical to always add new members. New additions also add fresh perspectives, and their voices keep the chapter meetings energized and exciting. Our method of bringing in new members follows a three-step process: identify, attract, and invite.

Identify—We all take on the responsibility for identifying Catholic business leaders, consultants, or professional people who have significant influence in the workplace. We strive to find someone who is serious about his faith and sees the WBC as a way to further his faith journey. This "identification" process continues when I (as the chapter leader) meet a prospect over coffee or lunch and involves me giving an overview of the purpose of WBC and determining if that aligns with his personal goals.

Attract—Once a prospect is identified and there is mutual interest, I give him a copy of Jim Nolan's book, *Doing the Right Thing at Work* and ask that we meet again in two to four weeks to discuss it. I also send him a few recaps of our recent meetings, as well as selected articles that will illustrate our purpose and the content of our meeting discussions. Reading and discussing the book has been by far the most effective way to help a prospect become interested in WBC.

Invite—Once the prospect has clearly indicated interest in joining the group, an invitation is extended to attend our next meeting. With one exception in two years, the experience of attending a meeting, participating in our vibrant discussions, and debriefing afterward has resulted in every prospect being excited about joining our chapter.

We are blessed to have a few resources that are significant in assisting our recruiting efforts. Our parish (and meeting place) is Saint Peter Chanel in Roswell, Georgia. Our pastor, Father Peter Rau, is very supportive (as was his predecessor, Father McNamee), and the deacon who heads our adult education programs, Deacon Mike Bickerstaff, is our chaplain. This strong parish-based support and sponsorship is a blessing and ensures that we have the appropriate Catholic focus on our efforts.

I have also led the Saint Peter Chanel Business Association ministry for the last few years. This group brings in monthly guest speakers to talk about their faith journeys and how they have integrated faith, family, and work. We also endeavor to provide sound education on Catholic teaching to the group through the meetings and monthly e-newsletter. In collaboration with Deacon Mike and Dr. Phil Thompson of the Aquinas Center of Theology at Emory University, I cofounded the first-ever Atlanta Catholic Business Conference in 2008, and each year it has been a big success. These ancillary groups and initiatives provide an ongoing source of candidates for our WBC chapter.

Building a Community

From the Atlanta chapter's beginning in August 2007, we have sought to build a strong sense of teamwork and community among our members. In order to achieve the necessary transparency and trust a successful meeting and chapter requires to build teamwork, we have purposefully pursued these evolving courses of action:

We meet informally outside of our monthly chapter meetings.

We each have a list of the group's contact information, and for the first few months of our existence we paired up people to get together for coffee or lunch with the desired purpose of building strong relationships in the chapter. Today, these informal meetings occur frequently with no guidance from me, and a strong bond amongst the group is the result.

We get our families together.

Our businesses are important, but our families are our primary vocation. We have enjoyed on a few occasions getting our families together for a cookout or meeting at restaurants. This makes our spouses more aware of our efforts and sets a good example for our children to see their parents in a group like WBC which has such noble goals.

We give back to the community.

Our group has always had a strong interest in stewardship and giving back to the community. Each quarter we identify a service project we can be involved in as a group. This has ranged from painting the home of a senior citizen, to feeding the homeless, to jointly sponsoring a table for the archdiocesan Saint Vincent de Paul Society fund-raising dinner. These activities give a strong sense of purpose to our efforts and bring the group closer together. We often bring family members to help with these service projects as well.

We pray for each other.

We end our meetings with a solicitation of special prayer requests from the group. We e-mail and call each other with these prayer requests as well. Prayer is vitally important to our Catholic faith, and we have made it central to our group as well.

One of the wonderful benefits to building a strong sense of community in our chapter is the desire we feel to help and support each other in any way possible. Be it a business issue, a family problem, or a faith-related dilemma, our members bend over backward to assist each other.

The Results (So Far)

The progress of our chapter in the last four years has been a real blessing. When we first got together in August 2007, we had grandiose ideas about being crusading Catholic business leaders and transforming the workplace. What we quickly discovered, however, was that we needed to transform ourselves from the inside before we could make a positive impact in the secular world. The desire to grow our interior lives, our prayer lives, and our relationships with Christ is the filter through which we conduct our meeting discussions.

This "course correction" early on took humility and the awareness that without surrendering to Christ (see Chapter 2) we can achieve very little in this life. The group members have, over time, become lights for Christ in the workplace who are attracting others by example, acts of selfless love, and the hopefully obvious fact that

Christ is at work in our lives. Our meetings are a constant revelation as we bring our workplace challenges up in discussion as well as the various successes that have come as a result of Christ at work in us. We pray that we will continue down this path and make a difference in the lives of those around us.

The Future

As we continue to grow our chapter, our focus going forward will also be on helping other chapters to get started in our Archdiocese and around the country. We have identified a few prospects, including one of our own members, who are interested in starting new chapters. We will continue to grow our membership and follow the effective guidelines of the Woodstock Business Conference to make a real difference in the workplace and help Catholics integrate their faith, family, and professional lives. All of this is possible through the guidance of the Holy Spirit, prayer, humility, and our sincere desire to serve others. Our members understand this very well, and I am grateful to be involved with such a dedicated group of Catholic professionals.

What we are attempting is a bit like discovering a new frontier. Transforming the workplace is a worthy apostolate, and the men and women we are encountering every day are largely enthusiastic about the idea of integration. They see a way to more deeply connect to their Catholic faith through the place where most of us spend the majority of our lives: the workplace.

For more information on the Woodstock Business Conference's mission, process, and additional resources, please visit: woodstock. georgetown.edu/programs/woodstock-business-conference.html.

APPENDIX 5

I Fall to My Knees

A Reflection on Eucharistic Adoration

In the True Presence of Christ, I fall to my knees.
I am humbled to be so near Him in the form of the Eucharist.
A feeling of peace and joy comes over me.
I start to pray in earnest because our Lord hears our prayers.
I offer Him my sincerest gratitude for the many blessings in my life.
I ask His forgiveness for the sins I have committed.
I promise our Lord that I will go to Reconciliation soon.
I unburden myself to Him and share all of my stress and anxiety
    as He asked us to in the Gospel.
I pray for others: family, friends, coworkers and anyone who is
    struggling or suffering.
I pray for the Church, the Holy Father and our Bishops,
    Priests, and Deacons.
I pray for our country and for our leaders to have moral courage
    and wisdom.
I pray for a world that will respect all life.
I pray that the Lord will make me a channel for His will today
    and every day.
Then I stop praying and I listen.

I listen for His voice.

Maybe He will speak to me through the friend I will encounter
that day or possibly in the meditation or Scripture passage
I am reading.

I go to Eucharistic Adoration out of love and devotion and
my passionate belief that this prayer time before the
Blessed Sacrament is the catalyst for my ongoing renewal
and conversion.

Go and spend time with Jesus today...He is waiting for you.

Quiet time before the Blessed Sacrament is an important and necessary part of a healthy prayer life and a critical part of our faith journeys as Catholics. To be in the same room with the Real Presence of our Lord and be humbled by his love and grace is an indescribable feeling. You have to experience it for yourself to truly understand. Our parish is blessed with perpetual eucharistic adoration, and many of our parishioners take full advantage of this incredible access to Christ to humbly seek him out at every opportunity for worship, prayer, and to unburden ourselves to him.

The *CCC* 1418 says: "Because Christ himself is present in the sacrament of the altar, he is to be honored with the worship of adoration. To visit the Blessed Sacrament is...a proof of gratitude, an expression of love, and a duty of adoration toward Christ our Lord" (Paul VI, *MF* 66).

In Pope John Paul II's apostolic exhortation, *On the Mystery and Worship of the Eucharist* (*Dominicae Cenae*), he lays out the case for eucharistic adoration:

"Adoration of Christ in this sacrament of love must also find expression in various forms of eucharistic devotion: personal prayer before the Blessed Sacrament, hours of adoration, periods of exposition—short, prolonged and annual (Forty

Hours)—eucharistic benediction, eucharistic processions, eucharistic congresses.

"The encouragement and the deepening of eucharistic worship are proofs of that authentic renewal which Vatican II set itself as an aim and of which they are the central point. And this...deserves separate reflection. The Church and the world have a great need of eucharistic worship. Jesus waits for us in this sacrament of love. Let us be generous with our time in going to meet him in adoration and in contemplation that is full of faith and ready to make reparation for the great faults and crimes of the world. May our adoration never cease."

As a convert to the Catholic Church, one of the first aspects of Catholicism that I had to understand and accept was the teaching on the Eucharist. As a Baptist in my teen years, we treated the Eucharist as a symbol and not the real body of Christ. As I was discerning about joining the Catholic Church in 2005, I was directed by a Catholic friend to read Christ's teaching of the Eucharist to his disciples in John 6:25–28, 48–58 and the Last Supper as told in Luke 22:14–20. As I read and reread these passages, I came to the obvious conclusion that Jesus was not speaking symbolically. He meant that the bread and wine were truly his Body and Blood. As this realization sunk in, so many other Catholic teachings began to make sense, but it was the recognition that the Catholic Church taught the true doctrine of the Eucharist that opened the way for me to convert. I share this with you because as Catholics we must believe truly and deeply with all our hearts that the Eucharist is the Body and Blood of Christ. This belief will allow us to more fully appreciate the blessings and gifts we have in holy Communion and eucharistic adoration.

Pope John Paul II pointed out in a homily he gave in 1979, "It is only by means of the Eucharist that we are able to live the heroic virtues of Christianity, such as charity to pardon one's enemies, the love which enables us to suffer, the capacity to give one's life for another; chastity at all times of life in all situations; patience in the face of suffering and the apparent silence of God in human history or our very own existence. Therefore always strive to be eucharistic souls so as to be authentic Christians."

It is a good idea to make a space on your calendar each week for an hour of eucharistic adoration in the pursuit of an "integrated life." It provides you with a respite from the busy workday to find peace with our Lord and worship in the Real Presence. It will make a profound difference on your faith journey as a Catholic if you practice this faithfully.

I have been a eucharistic guardian since January 2007, and this is the best hour of my week. To come into the Real Presence of Christ and thank him, pray to him, humble myself before him, and unburden myself to him puts my mind and heart at ease and prepares me for any challenge. I strongly encourage eucharistic adoration for everyone as a way to connect with Jesus in a deeper and more meaningful way.

Endnotes

1. *Christifideles Laici*, John Paul II, 17
2. Attributed to Saint Francis of Assisi
3. Motto of the Benedictine Order, *Catholic Book of Quotations*, Leo Knowles, p. 380
4. Saint Augustine, *Catholic Book of Quotations*, Leo Knowles, p. 226
5. Dr. Peter Kreeft, from the article "How Does the Weakness of the Cross Make Us Strong?" published on peterkreeft.com
6. Pope Benedict XVI, Mass for the Inauguration of the Pontificate of Pope Benedict XVI. Homily of his holiness Benedict XVI, Saint Peter's Square, April 24, 2005
7. The Suscipe, Saint Ignatius of Loyola, *Hearts on Fire: Praying With Jesuits*, p. 84
8. *Catechism of the Catholic Church*, 2744
9. Chris Lowney, quote from wharton.universia.net/index.cfm?fa =viewfeature&id=972&language=english
10. *Catechism of the Catholic Church*, 1827
11. *Stewardship: A Disciple's Response*, Introduction, p. 9, USCCB
12. *In Conversation With God*, Francis Fernandez, volume 4, p. 267-268
13. *Christifideles Laici*, John Paul II, 57–58
14. *Christifideles Laici*, John Paul II, 16

Other Related Liguori Publications Titles

How Can I Find God?
The Famous and the Not-So-Famous Consider
the Quintessential Question
James Martin

ISBN: 978-0-7648-0090-0

This vibrant collection brings together an array of voices addressing the question of how one might approach the search for God. With contributors from many faith traditions, this book will be of value to all who are seeking to answer the question, "How Can I Find God?"

Prayer in the Digital Age
Matt Swaim

ISBN: 978-0-7648-1979-7

Matt Swaim brings to light the obstacles to prayer inherent in our digitally connected culture and explores both the challenges and benefits of living a Christian life in the 21st century while providing practical suggestions for learning how to "unplug" and incorporate prayer into one's daily life.

Spiritual Blueprint
How We Live, Work, Love, Play, and Pray
James L. Papandrea

ISBN: 978-0-7648-1892-9

Author and lecturer James L. Papandrea helps you simplify your life, reduce stress, and understand your higher purpose by taking inventory and rebuilding the five "homes" of your life: Body, Hands, Heart, Mind, and Spirit. An integrated workbook walks you through the steps to identifying your strengths and weaknesses. If you're seriously interested in spiritual growth, changing negatives to positives, and reclaiming your higher purpose, *Spiritual Blueprint* is for you.